ACROSS THE GREAT DIVIDE

THIS BOOK IS DEDICATED TO THE CITIZENS OF DUNDEE
AND MY FAMILY, IN AND AROUND THE TOWN.
LOVE TO LORNA, EOGHAN AND JASMINE.

MAINSTREAM SPORT

ACROSS THE
GREAT DIVIDE

A HISTORY OF PROFESSIONAL
FOOTBALL IN DUNDEE

JIM WILKIE

MAINSTREAM
PUBLISHING

EDINBURGH AND LONDON

The author wishes to express his thanks to Flora McNeill (Glasgow/Uig), who typed above and beyond the call; the staff of the Dundee Library, Local History Room; the staff of the Mitchell Library (Glasgow), the Glasgow Room; Kevin McCarra; Pat Woods; George Hill; Lochee Harp; D.C. Thomson Photofiles; Donnie Coutts; the Scottish Football League (David Thomson); the Scottish Football Association (Marjory Nimmo); and the legendary Billy Kay.

First published in 1984 by
MAINSTREAM PUBLISHING (EDINBURGH) LTD
7 Albany Street
Edinburgh EH1 3UG

ISBN 1 84018 412 4

This edition 2000

A catalogue record for this book is available from the British Library

Typeset in Copperplate and Times
Printed and bound in Great Britain by Cox and Wyman Ltd

INTRODUCTION

If you were to describe the City of Dundee, probably the last word which would come to mind is 'beautiful'. More than likely you would use adjectives like 'grey', 'grim' even, 'industrial' or 'peculiar' – and Dundee certainly is an unusual city. For a start its history and dialect are unique – sub-cultural almost – but it's tucked away in an obscure corner of the Scotland's east coast, bypassed almost invariably by those heading north to the 'romantic' Scottish Highlands, or south to the 'glittering' conurbations. And you'd never call Dundonians romantic (or glittering). Hardened by centuries of economic and political uncertainty, their appearance and manner are often regarded as dour and uncompromising. Yet anyone who has spent any time actually living or working there knows that this is nothing like the whole story.

Dundee's splendid situation on the north bank of the Tay estuary can be seen to good advantage from Balgay Hill. And if that view of the old town at the foot of the Law, linked to the green hills of Fife by two spectacular bridges, with the promontory of Broughty Ferry beyond, doesn't strike a chord, then you might as well carry on looking, either for your fortune, or your Granny's Hielan' Hame.

One way or another, when Dundee United Football Club

won their first Scottish Premier League Championship in season 1982–83, the city was described by one of the country's best football writers, Ian Archer, as 'lonely, neglected and almost beleaguered'. It was true. Dundee, like everywhere else in Britain, was trying to combat the worst economic conditions for 50 years; that very week the large workforce of the Timex Electronics Company was under siege by a Tory government for daring to strike on a point of principle when the employment rate stood locally at 16 per cent; and the red, black, white and green flag which hung in the City Chambers acknowledged the achievements not of their now-famous footballing sons, but of the Palestine Liberation Organisation.

The city, of course, did pay handsome tribute to the club and players who brought such honour to it by winning the most keenly fought and thrilling Premier League competition since its inception, and civic chests swelled with additional pride, for this relatively small club had secured its victory with a pool, generally speaking, of 14 players, eight of whom came from the Tayside Region and seven from Dundee itself. Aberdeen FC, by comparison, with a city to themselves, oil rich and booming, won the European Cup-Winners' Cup some three days earlier with a pool of 16 players, only four of whom could be regarded as locals.

And Dundee United certainly do not have their hometown to themselves. Literally across the street from their ground, Tannadice Park, in the north end of the inner city stands Dens Park – in some ways a more imposing stadium which, for many years after its construction was the home of Dundee Football Club, cast something of a shadow over Tannadice. For whilst their rivals languished in the old Scottish Second Division for the greater part of the first 60 years of their existence, Dundee FC won every major trophy in the Scottish game, had a substantial number of their players capped for Scotland and reached a European Cup semi-final in 1963.

As surely as the seasons change, however, so too do footballing fortunes, and the early 1980s saw Dundee United finally and conclusively emerge from that shadow as a leading club, not only in Scottish, but in European football. And these things are important. Why else, for example, would anyone remember Jock Stein, Bob Shankly or Jim McLean?

Jim Wilkie
October 1984

* * *

It is very satisfying to be writing the introduction to a new edition of *Across the Great Divide*, especially when the original is now 16 years old. This means, of course, that there is a completely new generation of football fans in Dundee and I hope that, as they begin to grapple with the complexities of the modern game – Bosman, satellite TV, internet, boardroom extravaganzas . . . and all this before a ball is kicked – it might help to know something of the origins and history of professional football in their home town. In 1984 United had reached the European Cup semi-final and Dundee were threatening a revival under Archie Knox and Jocky Scott. Change was, of course, inevitable but no one could have predicted what form it would take.

J.W.
October 2000

ONE

Although there are no records, it can be assumed that some kind of football has been part of man's life for thousands of years. Classical Egyptian, Greek and Chinese literature contain explicit references to the sport – in one exotic Chinese version, teams vied with one another to score goals by kicking the ball through an opening in a silken net – and the Romans, who are said to have fostered football as part of their military training, are generally assumed to have brought the game to Britain. Football probably belongs to the category of primitive fertility rites, with the ball representing the sun or the head of an animal sacrifice and, given that reliable references to the game occur only after 1066, some believe the Normans developed it from the rites of Roman saturnalia (a feast concerned with fertility).

The first extensive description of British football dates from the London of 1175. It is an account by one William Fitzstephen of how, on Shrove Tuesday that year, the youth of the city spent part of the day cockfighting 'and in other boyish pursuits, and after dinner, they went to a local piece of ground . . . just outside the city for the famous game of ball'. Soon, authorities came to view the game as a nuisance and, as in the case of other sports, a danger to national security on the grounds that it interfered with the country's defence, in which efficiency with bows and arrows was most essential. There were other grounds, too, on which the authorities based their opposition of football, for the lack of any code often caused the games to degenerate into riotous running battles. This 'mob' or 'rough' football, as it was known, probably was not dissimilar to the famous 'Ba' game' which still persists in Kirkwall.

In 1314 King Edward II of England, following his humiliation at Bannockburn, where his archers were thought to have performed particularly badly, issued an edict forbidding football in his domain. Now, whereas it might be supposed the Scots would logically adopt the opposite viewpoint, and cultivate the warlike potential of their football, this proved not to be the case. Indeed, the game was also frowned upon by Scottish kings of the fifteenth century. In 1603, however, James VI of Scotland assumed the crown of a united Britain as James I ('the wisest fool in Christendom'), and football was again recognised, and even encouraged. By then, of course, archery had become redundant with the introduction of firearms, and by the nineteenth century the more refined and organised form of man's primitive kicking games were becoming popular everywhere. In this refinement and organisation, the educated classes played a prominent part.

In keeping with earlier aristocratic interest, 'rough' football was played at the English public schools, and playing it was one of the ways in which senior boys dominated others. During the 1830s and 1840s, however, the public schools – like several other important institutions – underwent reform and that included the reform of football. Also, many of the pupils wished to go on playing at university, and different schools had different ideas as to how the game should be played. It was at Cambridge University, first in 1848 and then in the 1860s, that experiments finally produced a body of rules which appeared to have a fairly wide acceptance, first in England and then in Scotland, where Queen's Park Football Club was established in 1867 and the Scottish Cup instituted in 1873. Eight teams competed for that first cup – Queen's Park, Clydesdale, Vale of Leven, Dumbreck, Third Lanark Volunteer Reserves, Eastern, Granville and Kilmarnock – and they effectively thus formed the Scottish Football Association. This was followed by the formation of the Scottish League in 1890, and the first League Handbook of 1981–82 listed a First Division of twelve clubs, Alliance of twelve, a Federation of twelve a Midland League of ten, an Ayrshire League of ten, and a Northern League of eight – three of whose members came from Dundee.

* * *

Dundee, in the late nineteenth century, was a textile town, with jute its most valuable commodity. Jute had come to Dundee for a variety of reasons: the uncertainty of flax supplies from territory controlled by Russia, with whom Britain had recently been at war; jute's relative abundance and cheapness; the impact of exceptional demand as a result of the aforementioned war, and the cotton famine of the 1860s; local technical progress in engineering; the willingness of Victorians to plough back profits; and the almost universal economic boom in the 1870s. All these factors served to stimulate expansion.

In 1839 the industry did not exist; in 1890, out of a total workforce (i.e. those in employment) of 80,000, more than 40,000 worked in jute, nearly all of them in or around Dundee. Perhaps the most astonishing thing, however, is that at least 30,000 of those were women and children (female labour being thought cheaper and more pliable than its male equivalent) and the result was the development of a kind of 'mill-girl culture' which would have touched most families in the town, and therefore been an important factor in the shaping of the Dundee character and way of life.

Textiles were not the only source of employment in the town, however. Shipbuilding and engineering were also major employers – although at this time printing and confectionery were not – and by the 1880s and 1890s, most working people had won the privilege of a Saturday half-day. Saturday afternoon, therefore, became a great time for 'true' leisure (as opposed to the 'enforced' leisure of unemployment) and a general interest in sports began to develop among the masses.

Initially, the geography of Dundee, with its steep, south-facing site, was not particularly suited to sport. But this began to change, since flat land was sought-after, for industrial premises as well as for sports grounds, and both the Harbour Road and Town Council were beginning to reclaim land. Indeed, the reclamation of Riverside Park (or the 'Cowp' as it is sometimes known) to the west of the Tay Bridge was begun at this time. It now, of course, also houses Dundee Airport.

There is no fixed date for when football first began in Dundee. A game called 'football' is first recorded as being played in the city in the early 1870s but this, as previously stated, was a time when Association Football was still in an experimental stage throughout Britain, and the (amateur) game which was played by the Dundee clubs bore a greater resemblance to present-day rugby than football, with opposition coming from 'good' schools and universities. Even at this, however, there was still some confusion, as a letter to the editor of the *Dundee Advertiser* of 17 January 1873 illustrates:

Sir,

The report in Monday's *Advertiser* of the football match played at St Andrews between the University team and those of Dundee and Broughty is not altogether correct. The match was to have been twenty a side, but the North of Tay only succeeded in mustering 14 players.

Four St Andrews men, however, were transferred to their side and the game was played eighteen a side. Your report should also have stated that an additional touch-down behind goal was claimed by the St Andrews team.

I am, etc.,

Joseph Brown,

72 North St, St Andrews.

In his footnote, a slightly rattled editor remarked: 'It seems impossible to get reports of these matches to which objection is not taken by some of the players.' How right he was.

Between 1874 and 1876, two clubs, one called Dundee United and the other Dundee, had fixtures at Blackness Park and Baxter Park respectively, playing rugby rules. But many experiments were taking place locally now, and the following year an *Advertiser* report (13 March 1877) referred to one side's 'splendid passing game which brought out the great superiority of the Association over the Rugby style of play'. The game, between Dunmore and Strathmore, was played 11 a side, with a goalkeeper, two backs, two half-backs and six forwards. In September of that year, the SFA meeting, with a Dundee representative present, announced that there were now 91 clubs in the Association, an increase of 23 since the previous year. Rugby and football were going their separate ways – and the operation was sometimes painful. In a match between Vale of Strathmore (Coupar Angus) and Dunkeld, which was theoretically played under Association rules, one of the Strathmore team had an arm dislocated, another bore 'visible marks of rough treatment' and a third was unable to finish the game. The *Advertiser* commented that the rules 'must have been disobeyed'.

In the west, however, the game was flourishing. Twenty thousand had watched Vale of Leven defeat Glasgow Rangers in the 1877 Scottish Cup final, and in 1878, Glasgow outfitters R.W. Forsyth began to advertise 'football costumes' in the Dundee newspaper. 'Jerseys, hose, belts, caps, cowls and knickerbockers' were all available by post from the Renfield Street shop which claimed to supply 'over 300 clubs'. This, more than anything else, confirmed that football was becoming big business throughout Central Scotland. By the end of the decade, at least three more clubs had added their name to the growing list in Dundee. They were Our Boys (founded 1877), East End (also founded 1877) and Dundee Harp, who were formed in 1879.

TWO

The last 20 years of the nineteenth century were traumatic for the British people. The Victorian era of expansion was drawing to a close and, curiously, an event in Dundee helped to bring this realisation home. On the night of Sunday, 28 December 1879, the high girders, or central section, of the Tay Bridge – at that time the longest railway bridge in the world – collapsed in a high wind, taking with them an engine, six coaches and 75 passengers. The event, according to historian John Prebble, shook the British Empire to its very foundations, since it destroyed the Victorians' smug pride and their belief in their own creative infallibility. One intrepid *Advertiser* reporter managed to keep his head, however. In the detached manner for which certain east coast newspapers were to become famous, he reported that a match played between Arbroath and Glasgow Wanderers on New Year's Day 1880 (i.e. four days after the disaster) 'was advertised to commence at 2.30 p.m. but owing to the Glasgow players having lost the connecting train at Dundee . . .' began late. 'A strong gale,' he continued, 'blew from the commencement of the match which towards the end increased almost to a hurricane.' What style!

The effect of this great trauma was a kind of preparation

for the new world which change was about to bring. The 1880s and 1890s also witnessed first the adoption of football by the working classes as their national game and then its transition from casual amateur status to organised professionalism and the object of a kind of religious fervour. Leisure time had been hard won and if the Victorian promise of eternal prosperity through hard work and faith in the Lord was not to be fulfilled then, metaphorically speaking, the freedom train was approaching Wormit and the wind was getting up . . .

It was then that men, in their frantic escapist search, first discovered the spiritual qualities of football – for although to play at the highest level was the achievement of few, it was the aspiration of many. Merely watching its matches brought a new kind of release, a new kind of solidarity and a new kind of sociability. Of course, the fact that there might be a job of work at the end of the line, or indeed a business investment, did not go entirely unnoticed.

At the beginning of the 1880s, however, the game was still strictly amateur and the quaint names of some of the local clubs bore testament to the Corinthian spirit. There were 'Perseverance', 'Try Again' and a particular favourite, 'Our Boys', with teams from Brechin, Blairgowrie, Arbroath, Dunfermline and Dundee all adopting that title. Originally it had been a nickname given to Glasgow Rangers during the 1870s and was probably the origin of the expression 'The Boys' as in 'C'mon the Boys!'. The first match between Our Boys (Dundee) and East End (Dundee) took place on Saturday, 24 February 1880. It was an occasion which was eagerly anticipated and the teams met on a local farmer's land, Lawton Park. Tapes were used instead of crossbars at the time. Our Boys won by two goals to nil. Their colours were red and black stripes with white shorts, but in 1882 they changed to the now more familiar dark blue jerseys and white shorts and acquired a 'home'

pitch at West Craigie Park, on farmland to the west of
Baxter Park. (The Tayside works later expanded northwards
to cover part of this ground and Morgan Place was built on
another part in 1937.) East End, meanwhile, who played in
blue and white stripes, made their home ground Clepington
Park near the present site of Tannadice and the Harp (green
jerseys, harp on breast, dark shorts) acquired their own Harp
Athletic Grounds in East Dock Street, near the large gas
tanks.

Both Harp and Hibernians (Dundee) had been
established to cater for the immigrant Irish population of
Dundee. In 1861, out of a population of approximately
100,000, between 14,000 and 15,000 were Irish-born
citizens attracted by the prospect of work in the rapidly
expanding jute industry. This was roughly the same
proportion as existed in Glasgow at the time, but whereas in
that city, or indeed Greenock, Edinburgh or Aberdeen, there
were more Irish males than females, in Dundee there were
twice as many women as men.

According to William Walker, author of *Juteopolis*, Dundee
appears to have attracted only the Catholic Irish. But the fact
that there were more women than men, that Dundee was a
Liberal 'frontier town' where anti-Irish prejudice would be no
more serious than, say, prejudice against Highlanders or
country folk from Fife or Angus and – perhaps most significant
– that membership of Orange Lodges was very small and
politically unimportant, went a long way to explaining the
relative absence of Irish sectarianism in the city. Also, socially,
the two nations which existed in Dundee were not Scots and
Irish, or Protestant and Catholic, but rich and poor for while
some inhabited mansions in the West End or Broughty Ferry,
virtually all the others shared the tenements in conditions
which were grim even by the standards of comparable
industrial towns. The infant death rate in these tenements was
ten times as high as in the suburbs, and the general physical,

moral and mental degradation contributed to the need for some kind of diversion and improvement. In 1873 the Catholic community, which by then owned a number of churches and schools, acquired a 'Young Men's Hall' in Tay Street. This was designed for the purposes of recreation and education and was said to be the finest in Dundee. It was therefore but a short step to establish a football club with its own grounds.

The Forfarshire Football Association was formed in 1883 at the initiative of the leading Dundee clubs and consisted in its first season of 18 teams – twelve from Dundee, two from Arbroath, one each from Montrose, Broughty Ferry and Lochee (the 'dark village' which was slowly being converted by the jute-owning Cox family into an industrial suburb) and one from Coupar Angus, two of whose forwards went by the name of Gilzean. The first Forfarshire Cup was won by Arbroath, who defeated Harp 2–1 in the final, and when another cup was presented to the Association by the Dundee Burns Club, local rivalry became greatly intensified.

Our Boys and East End were the clubs which made the early running with each turning out up to three teams a week, but the real success story was that of Harp whose hat-trick of Forfarshire Cup victories in the 1880s (1884–85, 1885–86, 1886–87) earned them the nickname 'The Invincibles' in the Glasgow press. The standard of football, however, was still lower than in the west, for although they reached the fourth round of the Scottish Cup in 1884–85, they lost 6–0 to Vale of Leven. On the east coast, though, they ranked second only to Edinburgh Hibs at this time (Dundee Hibs were erased from the SFA roll before season 1884–85) and whereas many schoolboys know that the record score in Scottish football is Arbroath's 36–0 defeat of Bon Accord (Aberdeen) on 12 September 1885, how many know that the second-highest score was achieved by Harp in the same round of the Scottish Cup? That same Harp beat Aberdeen Rovers 35–0 and, according to the Scottish press, it could have been more! At least Aberdonians can take some comfort from the fact that, 100 years on, footballing standards in their home town have improved somewhat.

The year 1885 must go down as one of the most significant in the city of Dundee's footballing history. The week after their record-breaking performance, Harp met Our Boys at East Dock Street in the second round of the Forfarshire Cup. The 'bible' of Scottish sport, the Glasgow-based *Scottish Umpire*, compared the crowd of 10,000 to that at an international, and in losing 3–1 to their great rivals, Our Boys must have been bitterly disappointed. So much so, in fact, that some two months later, deep-seated differences between the players and the committee came to the surface and resulted in a strike by Our Boys' players against their committee, with the players demanding the resignation of the 'old and popular president' of the club, Mr J.M. Dron. The committee, however, held firm, and when two players – Buttars and Porter – changed their minds, a new team was quickly assembled around them.

But the damage was done, with the result that the other players severed their connection with the club and started a new combination under the name of the 'Wanderers'. Their nickname was 'The Forkies', possibly because they had 'forked off' from Our Boys. The *Scottish Umpire* commented that 'the plucky management of "the Boys" committee will remain as a standing memorial of what a few able and right-minded men can do'. Revolution, it would seem, was not popular with the editor, who went on to remark that even the very name chosen by the new club was a 'suggestive sobriquet'. Whatever might be in a name, however, this rift was to prove bitter, irreconcilable and – arguably – the historical basis of Dundee's development as a divided footballing city.

First of all, the struggle for pre-eminence in the town

became a four-cornered one between Our Boys, East End, Wanderers and Harp, but this was increasingly overshadowed by a new factor. For as clubs broadened their appeal, more and more people began to identify with one or other particular team. As the pressure to win increased, so did the competition for the best local players and this in turn led to clubs paying the best players to come and play for them. Thus the small local clubs were forced along a road to professionalism which was legalised first in England in 1885.

Professionalism existed in other sports at the time, notably boxing and cycling, but it had a bad reputation owing to the gambling it attracted. Professional cricket, however, had managed to maintain its dignity and this became the model for English clubs faced with the issue. Soon the top English clubs were visiting Scotland for holiday fixtures at New Year or Easter and this in turn led to the first wholesale plundering of Scottish football by their wealthy neighbours.

The SFA initially stood firmly against what it called the 'unmitigated evil of professionalism' and 'even Parnell', said the *Scottish Umpire*, 'could not have uttered more acrid denunciations against the land of the rose'. The Scottish football establishment more or less got its own way until season 1890–91 when a case of professionalism was proved against St Bernards of Edinburgh and they were suspended for six weeks. It was the opinion of the SFA that the club then simply made a few cosmetic changes and changed their name to Edinburgh Saints; so when Renton (Champions of the World, 1888) applied to play the Saints, permission was refused. Renton, however, went ahead and both clubs were expelled, which meant that they were effectively banned from the new Scottish League too. Renton sued the SFA and achieved an out-of-court victory which resulted in an amnesty for professionals in Scotland.

Of course, the whole thing was a sham in that players throughout the country were being paid. But given that, the Dundee club had suffered very badly as a result of English professionalism, and none worse than Harp, whose match secretary, a Mr James Diamond, believed that if they had all their English players reinstated, they would be one of the best clubs in Scotland. Replying to a *Scottish Sport* (*Scottish Umpire* became *Scottish Sport* in 1888) editorial on Dundee which railed against disgraceful grounds, petty personal dignities, club jealousies and – significantly – the fact that there were too many senior clubs in the town (the editor suggested two), Diamond stated that it was not the number of clubs but the activities of the 'English agent' which prevented Dundee clubs from taking their rightful place at the top of the table of Scottish football. Indeed, he suggested then that an amnesty would be the best course of action.

Mr Diamond and his club had had a difficult few years. In January 1887, when still the best team in Forfarshire, Harp were involved in an incident which served to blacken their reputation. Having been drawn away to a leading west coast club, Dumbarton, in the third round of the Scottish Cup, Harp elected to scratch; but, expecting a good gate, they offered Dumbarton a £20 guarantee to play the match as a friendly in Dundee. Dumbarton agreed and, anticipating the usual 12.45 p.m. kick-off, were surprised to learn just after noon, as they sat in their hotel, that the kick-off time was in fact 12.15 p.m. The players rushed to the ground, but when they arrived they discovered that Harp had told the (small) crowd that Dumbarton had failed to turn up and had given them their money back. To make matters worse, the game had been advertised as the Scottish Cup tie and when the *Umpire* raised the point, Diamond blamed the misunderstanding on his superiors who, he claimed, would not allow him to take the words 'Scottish Cup 3rd round' off the bills. In any event, the

Harp executive, including Diamond, were dismissed. The *Umpire* mercilessly pursued the club and its 'inner circle' through its columns for the next few years by continually alluding to the incident.

Harp now went into a period of decline and in 1890 another stick was found with which to beat them. Glasgow Celtic were founded in 1887–88 and, like Harp, were initially a sectarian club inasmuch as all their players and officials were Roman Catholics (mostly of Irish origin). Celtic were founded as a charity for the relief of the poor in Glasgow's east end, but in the 1890s commercial pressures dictated that they become first a limited liability company and then that they sign the best players irrespective of their religion or background. In 1895, a motion was put forward that the number of Protestants in the team should be limited to three, but this was defeated by a counter-motion that the committee should have the right to sign as many Protestants as they wished. From that day forth, Celtic Football Club has been a non-sectarian organisation.

In the late 1880s, the issue of sectarianism in sport did not appear to concern the establishment, or at least the editor of the *Umpire*: 'We learn,' he wrote in November 1887, 'that the efforts which have lately been made to organise a first-class Catholic Club have been consummated. We wish the Celts all success.' This attitude, however, was to change and the change coincided with Celtic's rapid rise to prominence. By November 1890, when they visited Our Boys (Dundee), Celtic were one of Scotland's leading clubs, and the occasion was described as the 'most important event . . . in the history of Northern football'. A crowd of 4,000 saw Celtic defeat the 'Blues' 3–1 at West Craigie, where for the first time a special room had been set aside for the press. Not least impressed by this new (sectarian) club were the powers behind Harp.

Discouraged by the loss of nine players to England that

year, the Harp executive had taken a decision to play a 'mixed' XI of Scots and Irish in an attempt to restore the club's fortunes, and a new secretary, Charles Mulholland, had been appointed in September 1890 for the forthcoming season. Following the great impression which Celtic made, however, this policy was thrown overboard, the Scots players were abandoned and at a meeting of members and supporters on 26 November 1890 an effort was made to reorganise the club.[1] Senior officials, the Rev. Monsignor Clapperton, Rev. Fathers Holder, Harris and Van de Rydt decided 'that the club should in future be run on the same principle as Celtic' and a telegram was received from Celtic wishing them every success under their new management.

Scottish Sport commented: 'With such an Irish constituency as that to be found in Dundee, we can imagine no better field for a first-class Irish team and with the influence of the Roman Catholic clergy at its head, its sectarian success can be almost assured.' Now whether this prospect caused him a sleepless night is uncertain, but the editor followed this three days later with a rather different editorial. He began by outlining the history of the club and its recent (chequered) past, but said that he believed the right men had now come forward. The new honorary presidents were Fathers Holder and Harris, and Diamond had been reinstated as the match secretary. It was his conclusion, however, which was of particular interest:

> While we welcome the reconstruction of the Harp, we are sorry that it has been deemed advisable to run the management under the patronage of the church. We do not believe in clubs formed on sectarian lines; it does the cause of religion more harm than good and it brings the charity and humanity of sport into a narrow channel for the outflow of tolerance and the coarse feelings of our

everyday life. The Harp, by following the lines of Celtic, are introducing into Dundee and the north of Scotland, a phase of football which we happen to know does not have the sanction or support of some of the finest and most Catholic minds of the Romish church.

On 6 December 1890, Harp turned out an entirely 'Irish' team for the first time in almost a year. In front of a poor crowd, they defeated Strathmore 1–0.

NOTES

[1] Another factor which would have influenced the churchmen in their decision to become involved in the running of the Harp club was the storm which was then raging over Parnell's leadership of Sinn Fein. Following great success, Parnell was cited in a divorce case and the Catholic Church came down heavily in favour of his resignation. Perhaps they felt it was their duty to try to ensure that their moral values were upheld by the young Catholic community in the town. With a few notable exceptions, Presbyterian and Episcopalian ministers paid little attention to football and some openly opposed it.

THREE

The issue of sectarianism has never dominated football in Dundee and so it was in the Juteopolis at this time. East End (the 'Wise Men') reached the sixth round of the Scottish Cup in season 1989–90 and won the Burns Cup. And Our Boys went with them all the way, taking the Forfarshire goblet in 1889–90 and 1890–91. For the first time (though not the last) there were rumblings of favouritism by the SFA for west coast clubs when it came to handing out international 'caps' and no case was more spectacular than that of William Dickson (Strathmore) who was the first footballer from a Dundee club to play for Scotland. Dickson was in fact a Fifer from Crail who became a top-class centre-forward with Strathmore and, following some pressure by the *Umpire*, was picked to play against Ireland in 1888. In a 10–2 victory, he scored no fewer than four goals but, perhaps unremarkably, was never selected again. In a distinguished career he then moved to Sunderland, Aston Villa (he was an FA Cup finalist in 1892) and finally Stoke, with whom he was a player, coach and, ultimately, a director. Dickson was the first real football personality in Dundee and when he returned during close seasons, his movements were eagerly followed by the press who reported him once as having been spotted 'fishing for flooks' at Invergowrie. One can't see Charlie Nicholas having the same interest in flat fish, but if he did it would doubtless have been put before the public and with the same justification in the 1980s as the 1890s.

Meanwhile, Wanderers were managing to establish themselves alongside the 'bigger' clubs locally. Having made their home Morgan Park (off Mains Loan and connected to Morgan Academy, or Hospital, as it was in 1886, a boarding school for fatherless boys), they opened a grandstand there in season 1887–88 and reached the quarter-finals of the Scottish Cup. They also won the Burns Cup in 1886–87 and 1887–88 and at least three of their players, Henry, Duncan and Moodie, joined the exodus south. In December 1890, however, they faced a challenge of a different nature. Alex Batchelor, a farmer of West Craigie estate, which housed Morgan Park, sued the club for £28 as rent in arrears. A decree in absence was pronounced with the proviso that if security was obtained within a fortnight, the club would have three months in which to pay their debt. It would seem the matter could not be satisfactorily resolved, however, for Wanderers lost the tenancy of Morgan Park and moved to Clepington Park, which had been vacated in turn by East End when they moved to Pikterro Park, near the present home of Stobswell Juniors. In the early months of the following year, 1891, as if to make a fresh start, the club changed its name to Johnstone Wanderers[1] and at a meeting of the Dundee Burns Charity Association on 3 March the 'new' club was represented by a Mr J. Gamble.

By this time the highly successful Scottish League was reaching its first climax (Dumbarton and Rangers would share the first championship) and the formation of a Northern League was proposed since the leading Scottish clubs were now only visiting the north at New Year, and the game was deteriorating locally – although another Forfarshire player, the Dundee-born Alex Keillor (Montrose), was about to receive his first cap, against Wales. The first general meeting of the Northern League was held in Mather's Temperance Hotel (now the Tay Hotel) on Saturday, 4 April 1891. A Mr Duncan (Our Boys), seconded by Mr Spalding of East End, suggested a league of eight clubs. Mr Diamond of Harp, however, seconded by Mr Gamble of Johnstone Wanderers, suggested ten as both these clubs feared they might be excluded if only eight were elected. Their fears were well founded, for only three Dundee clubs were to gain admission and in the ballot Harp defeated Johnstone Wanderers by 14 votes to 6. The clubs elected were Montrose, Arbroath, Forfar Athletic, Our Boys, East End, Harp, St Johnstone and Aberdeen, and the exclusion of Johnstone Wanderers rather surprised the editor of *Scottish Sport*. Although the voting suggested that blame for this could not entirely be laid at Our Boys' door, he concluded that the 'old hatred' seemed likely to be rekindled and that Johnstone Wanderers would vow vengeance 'on the heads of those who were instrumental in procuring their exclusion'. They did not allow this vow to interfere with their progress, however, and in an attempt to keep up with East End – who now leased a new recreation ground at Carolina Port from the Harbour Trustees – they embarked on an ambitious scheme to improve Clepington Park.

The new ground was to be opened on 2 May 1891, with a game against Broughty Ferry, but the 'fireside sailors' failed to turn up and Clepington Park retained its virgin charms until the following week, when Raith Rovers did the honours. 'Like Morgan Park,' said *Scottish Sport*, 'the new enclosure has a slope but not nearly so pronounced.' There was no grandstand, but 'plenty of room for one' and, 'everything considered', the Wanderers were 'to be congratulated on having secured such comfortable quarters after encountering so many difficulties'. The park was opened by Bailie Stevenson and by the kind of coincidence that makes life interesting, that same week a young Dundee junior team, Strathmore Athletic, announced that they had decided to give themselves the somewhat pretentious title of Dundee United. The new stadium at Clepington Park, of course, was to become the home of the 'real' Dundee United, Tannadice Park.

Season 1891–92, the second of the Scottish League and the first of the Northern League, was also the first season of the professional amnesty. It made little difference to the flow of players south, but some technical improvements were being made in the way the game was played, in the field of play, and in the rules of the game. Over the next few years, football would begin to look more like the thing we know today, with the introduction of crossbars and goal-nets, the number of opponents in the offside rule being established as three, the penalty kick being introduced and 'hacking' outlawed. Players still had to 'claim' for a foul or goal, however, which would stand if one of the 'umpires' (linesmen) raised his stick and the referee blew his whistle. There was still no penalty box, merely a 12-yard line.

East End moved into the Carolina Port ground and Strathmore into Logie Park in Scott Street. Our Boys were offered exemption from the Scottish Cup but chose to play (against Harp) and lost 2–0. In a reported incident which reflects the depth of feeling between the clubs and also the social habits of the supporters in an age long before television the Wanderers' players, on returning to Dundee from their game in Perth, 'went to a corner in High Street' which was 'sacred to Our Boys and their supporters' and shouted, 'Three cheers for the Harp!'. (Supporters apparently would wait in High Street near the telegraph office in Thorter Row for results of their team's match, with each set having their own place.) The same issue of *Scottish Sport* also welcomed the Harp revival and in yet another about-face wrote: 'As an improving factor, there is nothing in Dundee to equal a successful Irish organisation.' In spite of these inconsistencies, however, it was not above reproaching others for unprofessional conduct. D.C. Thomson's *Courier* came under fire in the 1880s for plagiarising the *Umpire*'s Dundee notes; and the *Evening Telegraph* was later criticised for abandoning its 'Sporting Pink' over the summer months. 'Dundee,' said the *Umpire*, 'deserved better.'

Some other social comments from this publication also give an insight into contemporary life. 'Football Special' trains, for example, were begun in the 1880s and 1890s, although sometimes players themselves could not get to matches if they had to work on a Saturday. As if to remind the historian that this really was a different time, and the end of an era, *Scottish Sport* in November 1891 advertised the forthcoming appearance of none other than Buffalo Bill, whose Wild West Show played at the East End Exhibition Hall in the city's Duke Street.

Football was an even bigger attraction, however, and even the prospect of increased admission charges from 3d to 4d or 6d did not have any deterrent effect. At the time, a 'big offer' to a Dundee player (Dundas, Our Boys) from a top English club (Sheffield Wednesday) was £3.10s a week. Celtic won the 1891–92 Scottish Cup, Dumbarton the League, and the first Northern League championship was shared by Our Boys and East End. It was also decided to increase the Northern League membership from eight to ten clubs and Johnstone Wanderers and Victoria United (Aberdeen) were elected for season 1892–93. In 1892 Lochee United (who were said to have a close relationship with Harp) opened their new ground near South Road and could field a team entirely of Lochee men. They were looked upon as a senior team at this time and junior clubs like East Craigie and Violet were the province of younger players.

Leading the field in terms of amenities were East End, whose new ground at Carolina Port was comparable to anything in the west and able to accommodate 1,500 people in the stand, 1,000 at the rail, and up to 10,000 on the bank. The pitch itself was also splendid, with separate running and cycle tracks. And they had a team to match. Following a 5–1 victory against Our Boys, their goalkeeper, Ure, was 'courted' by the West Craigie club, where it was said he would meet 'fellows like himself – travellers, clerks etc. – which would be far better than mixing with such a common rough lot as the Carolina Port crowd'. Our Boys obviously considered themselves a better 'class' of team, but Ure stayed put. There was no shortage of money to keep him there, for at a home friendly match against Sunderland, the 'gate' was a staggering £104, from a 3d admission charge.

The issue of professionalism in Scotland now really began to gear up and Johnstone Wanderers, not to be left behind, built a grandstand at Clepington Park. Gates were said to be decreasing at the turn of the year, however, due to dull trade, bad weather, and the number of friendlies the local teams played against each other. When Our Boys' stand at West Craigie Park burned down, football in the town hit something of a low ebb. By the spring, though, all this was changing.

On 24 March 1893, *Scottish Sport* contained a report:

> Communications have been passing between two leading Dundee clubs over amalgamation and asking admittance to the Scottish League. At present the matter is being kept as secret as possible but from small indications observed, there is little chance of it being successfully carried out.

30

The two clubs were Our Boys and East End and the suggestion prompted a great deal of talk locally. The general opinion was that any other two clubs might unite and work in harmony, but that Our Boys and East End never could. Nothing, however, is certain in football and events now overtook opinion in Dundee.

At a revolutionary meeting of the SFA on 2 May 1893, the legislation of professionalism was proposed by the dynamic Mr J. McLaughlin of Celtic. Professionalism existed, he said, and everyone knew it, and in a revealing rejoinder he added that as things stood, players were masters of clubs. With the advent of professionalism, he argued, 'Clubs would not be masters of players and standards would rise . . . whether or not they approved of professionalism they should control it.' The motion was seconded by J. Gamble of Johnstone Wanderers and passed. 'Exit bogus amateurism,' said *Scottish Sport* in another fantastic U-turn, 'enter honest professionalism.'

The majority of the Forfarshire clubs were against legislation, as they thought the struggling clubs would be ruined, but in Dundee incredulity concerning the amalgamation was giving way to pragmatism and supporters of both clubs now focused their attention on what most were beginning to see as a positive, indeed lifesaving, move. There were dissenters, of course, but the officials of the two clubs continued to hold discussions. East End at that time were favourites to win the Northern League and had to beat Harp in the final game of the season to take the flag (20 May 1893). They lost 4–2. The all-conquering, all-local Arbroath team of that year beat them into second place, with Harp fifth, Johnstone Wanderers seventh and Our Boys eighth out of ten.

That evening an application was drafted for presentation at the Scottish League AGM on Monday, 12 June:

We, the undersigned as representing the Our Boys and East End clubs of Dundee, hereby make application for admittance as an amalgamated club to be named the Dundee Football Club to membership of the Scottish Football League.

We beg to submit that this application on behalf of the two leading clubs of this district has the entire sympathy of the general public and that committees and players of both clubs are prepared to give the new club their support.

Should this application receive your favourable consideration, we would point out to you the advantages financially of the scheme. Matches between local clubs at threepence for admission have drawn over £100 at the gates and we feel sure that with the admission raised to sixpence, and with interest attaching to a national competition such as the Scottish League, that this sum could be easily doubled.

One visit per annum from each of the league clubs would revive interest in the game here and would ensure large attendances.

Dundee, being the third largest centre of population in Scotland, viz 200,000 will, we think, commend itself favourably to you as a centre for a Scottish League club.

Dundee is now within easy reach of Edinburgh and Glasgow having connections with both the Caledonian and North British Railways. There is at the disposal of the new club a ground with a playing pitch of 120 yards long by 75 yards broad, quite level and well turfed. Accommodation is provided for 20,000 spectators.

We are certain that we can sustain the interest in
the competition throughout the entire season, as
we have a large field in the North of Scotland from
which to engage players to compose our team.

Signed   Wm Black
           Thomas Shaw   *East End FC*
           Andw Williamson
           John Cameron   *Our Boys*

[A. Buttar also signed the original document]

Amalgamation hinged on admission to the Scottish League,
and *Scottish Sport*[2] commented that the application should
be supported. When the news arrived in Dundee on the
Monday night that the new club was in at the head of the
League poll, any reservations which the respective
supporters had were magically dissolved and some even
danced in the High Street! The *Dundee Advertiser* marked
the occasion with the following report:

On Monday, 12 June 1893, the Annual General
Meeting of the Scottish Football League was held
in Glasgow. The balance sheet showed a large
surplus, and the office-bearers were all re-elected.
Thereafter, the representatives of Renton,
Abercorn and Clyde – the clubs which had fewest
points – retired, and applications for admission
were made by St Bernards and Hibernian
(Edinburgh) and the newly formed Dundee. The
final division resulted in an equal number of votes
being given for Renton and Dundee, while the last
vacancy went to St Bernards. The Scottish League
first division now comprised Celtic, Rangers,
Third Lanark, St Mirren, Dumbarton, Renton,

> Hearts, St Bernards, Leith Ath. and Dundee. Mr William Black represented the newly admitted club from the north.

The editor then opined:

> The new step will doubtless give a great impetus to the sport in Dundee. The new club has been formed by the amalgamation of Our Boys and East End, the object being to raise a team which, while thoroughly representative, will be capable of upholding the city's honour in the football field and which will be able to take a front place in the national competition.

Suitably Victorian sentiments, and the writer also remarked that the other nine clubs would in future have to come to Dundee in 'full strength' and not – as apparently had often been the case with friendly fixtures in Dundee – with a weak team. He concluded that Dundonians 'will next season have opportunities of witnessing all the most famous Scottish exponents of the game'.

Dundee had arrived as a footballing city.

NOTES

[1] A club called Johnstone Athletic had played at Fairmuir. The name may have related to a local estate or farm.

[2] *Scottish Sport* carried the following report in their edition of 23 June 1893:
  'The Dundee FC is now an accomplished fact. A general meeting of the East End was held on Monday night when it was resolved to wind up their affairs and join with Our Boys to form the new body. Six members

were chosen to represent them, and these gentlemen and their representatives met representatives of Our Boys on Tuesday evening (20 June) in Mather's Hotel, and the office-bearers in the new club were elected. The principle of election carried out was to choose members from the two clubs alternatively to fill the various offices. The following is the list:

President; James Petrie (East End)

Vice-president: A. Buttar (Our Boys)

Business Secretary: W. Black

Match Secretary: A. Williamson

Joint Treasurers: J. MacLean and J.M. Forbes

Sel. of A team: D. MacVicar

Committee: T. McKee, A. Spalding, W. Saunders, J. MacIntosh, W.K. Murray.

FOUR

Welcome! thrice welcome! to the year 1893,
For it is the year that I intend to leave Dundee.
Owing to the treatment I receive
Which does my heart sadly grieve.
Every morning when I go out
The ignorant rabble they do shout
'There goes mad McGonagall!'
In derisive shouts as loud as they can bawl
And lifts stones and snowballs, throws them at me;
And such actions are shameful to be heard in the
City of Dundee.

– New Year's Resolution to leave Dundee
William McGonagall,
b. Edinburgh 1825 *d*. Edinburgh 1903

Season 1893–94 was the first played in Scotland under professionalism and all in all it was deemed a great success. For the next few years, however, patrons in Dundee might have been excused for thinking they were at the Gussie Park Carnival rather than their favourite football ground, such was the merry-go-round of soccer in the city. Harp, for example, while accepting professionalism, felt they simply could not afford to pay players unless the home club received all the gate-money and they put forward a motion to that effect at a special meeting of the Northern League. Further, they required an increase in admission charges to 4d for adults and 2d for juveniles – but it was generally recognised that only the second proposal would receive the sanction of the committee and so the feeling was that Harp's letter was effectively one of resignation. Indeed, Mr Diamond had gone so far as to state that they 'were not anxious to enter the League' that season and, although they recruited some new men from the west, they eventually decided to resign and were replaced by Strathmore.

Strathmore was thought to be the oldest surviving football club in the town and they proceeded to cause a minor sensation by securing the lease of Carolina Port, which had been expected to go to the new amalgamation. Dundee FC, therefore, began life in the rather less auspicious surroundings of West Craigie Park. But this in no way detracted from the sense of occasion at the opening match against Glasgow Rangers on Saturday, the 'glorious twelfth' of August 1893. There was great excitement in the town and by two o'clock the crowd was streaming along Arbroath Road. Ultimately, between 4,000 and 5,000 people assembled and they apparently got good value for their 6d admission fee, witnessing a 3–3 draw. Dundee lined up: McKie, Ferrier, and Brown; Craig, Longair and Petrie; Thomson, Craik, Dundas, Gilligan and Keillor (the international 'cap' who had joined from Montrose). The *Advertiser* commented: 'Thus has Dundee been successfully launched on its League career.'[1]

West Craigie Park was not a long-term proposition, however, and following a number of defeats, the Dundee committee decided to stage a business 'coup' by buying a controlling interest in the Athletic Grounds Company which was in financial difficulty. This put Strathmore in an invidious position and early in 1894 they decided to amalgamate with Johnstone Wanderers at Clepington Park in an attempt to provide the city with a second top-class club. The name they chose for the new combination was Dundonians FC but Dundee FC objected, claiming, understandably, that they were already being referred to in the national press as 'the Dundonians'. Otherwise, however, Dundee FC were said to welcome the new amalgamation and when their objection was upheld by the SFA, the Clepington Park club decided to opt for the 'Wanderers' as their name. Their colours were red and white shirts and blue shorts.

Harp, meanwhile, who themselves had long harboured ambitions of becoming a top club, were slipping farther into difficulty through mismanagement and a failure to meet their financial obligations to other clubs. On 3 April 1894 they were suspended by the SFA for non-payment of guarantees. There was immediately a rumour that a new Irish club might appear in the hands of men of 'higher social standing' and in September 1894 such a club did appear – to be known as the Dundee Hibs. In order to circumvent the stigma which attached in official circles to the name Harp, a statement was issued that none of the executive of the defunct club was on the committee of the new organisation, and with the following officials the club set up home at West Craigie: president, John Fagan; vice-president, J. Flood; financial secretary, P. Doyle; treasurer, J. MacLaren; match secretary, Frank Carroll.

Wanderers (represented by president, D. Reid; vice-president, J. Duncan; joint treasurers, J. Alexander and J. McCulloch; financial secretary, D. MacEwan; and match secretary, J. MacLeod) were also elected to the new Scottish Second Division in 1894. But they ran into trouble almost immediately by losing the tenancy of Clepington Park and although they found a new home at East Dock Street (Harp's old ground), their bad luck did not abate – when they finished second bottom of the Second Division, they failed to be re-elected. Dundee FC, however, continued to put up a good performance in the First Division and finished eighth of ten in each of their first two seasons. Relations had also improved between the two clubs to such an extent that Dundee actually loaned their old rivals money at one stage – a gesture thought noteworthy by the Glasgow press – and in signing the ex-Harp goalkeeper, Francis Barrett, the club showed an immediate willingness to go for the best players, whatever their religion. Besides, it was good business to have a popular 'Irishman' in the side and Barrett went on to become one of Dundee FC's first international 'caps', along with Longair and Keillor, for Scotland against Ireland in 1894.

The 1894–95 season also saw Dundee's first successful Scottish Cup run. Having defeated the mighty Celtic in an earlier round and for record gate-money, the Dark Blues went on to contest an epic, three-match semi-final with Renton before finally going down 3–0.[2] The returns, and not for the last time, showed the club the financial value of a good run in the Scottish Cup, but even this much-needed finance and success was not enough to enable them to hold on to their star centre-forward Maxwell. He was enticed by a local scout to join Dickson at Stoke, and went on to become the first Dundonian to play for Scotland against England, in 1898.

So the 'carnival' continued. Wanderers returned to Clepington Park. Dundee Hibs became Harp again in 1895, had the name ratified by the SFA at the second attempt and moved back to Dock Street. And Dundee FC witnessed serious hooliganism for the first time. Following a game with Hearts at Tynecastle on 2 November 1895, a crowd of about 1,000 Hearts supporters congregated outside the pavilion to remonstrate with a young Dundee forward called

Vail, whose robust challenges had not met with their approval. Police were called and had to draw batons while Vail made his exit through the back door. It was said to be the first incident of its type in Edinburgh and the Hearts officials regretted it 'exceedingly'.

The fact that clubs could pay the price of admission to the 'show', therefore, did not guarantee a joyride, and Dundee FC were next to experience the effects of the roundabouts and swings of professionalism. Although they were having their best season so far, there were indications of a cash crisis at Carolina Port shortly after New Year 1896, and one or two guarantees were said to be outstanding. The problem, said the *Sport*, was that although Dundee had done well in the League (they were to finish fifth in the First Division that season), they were out of the Scottish Cup. With no prospects of lucrative friendlies against local rivals because of the inferiority of the opposition, the club had only its traditional holiday fixtures against English opposition to look forward to, and this could not pay the wages. The Glasgow paper, therefore, again called for a strong new club in the town and again it demonstrated its ambivalence on the issue of sectarianism. 'If the new body has sectarian flavour,' declared the editor, 'so much the better, as the Irish population in Dundee is a very large one.' This institutionalised ambivalence has continued to afflict the Scottish game. On the one hand sectarianism in sport is condemned while, on the other, if it is seen to do no harm to a club's commercial prospects, it is overlooked or even justified. At least it can be said that the Dundee clubs made some kind of attempt to resolve this dilemma (although some people would have liked Dundee FC in particular to go farther) and, in fairness, the *Sport* recognised even then that, whatever a club's policies, it still has to produce a first-class team to enjoy success.

At a meeting of the committee on 27 January 1896,

Dundee FC told their players that their wages were to be reduced. The club was not in immediate danger, but future payments were such that if expenses were not cut forthwith then trouble would be inevitable. There was talk of a players' revolt, but in the end only one player, the captain, Hendry, changed clubs as a result of the edict. The rent for Carolina Port was also causing problems and Dundee were said to have their eye on a new field in the north end of the town – but not before the 'Burning Mountain' (a shale bing near the Carolina Port ground which continued to smoulder) had its moment of glory when it formed the backdrop for the Scotland–Wales international played at Carolina Port in March 1896. The pitch was said to be in poor condition for the game, but the large crowd were well disciplined, and the *Sport* once again called for a 'second' team in Dundee, this time an amalgamation of Wanderers and Harp.

It was the city's 'first' team, however, which was causing immediate concern, and matters came to a head on 23 April when a revolutionary group emerged at the Dundee AGM to launch an assault on the embattled committee. President Brown and vice-president Kidd, as non-party members, managed to hold on to their positions, but only two members of the old committee survived with them: the names of Williamson, Black and Petrie were replaced by Ireland, Andrews and Smellie. The first reaction of the old guard was to throw their lot behind the Wanderers and an application for membership of the Second Division went before the SFA on behalf of a new club, Dundee County. It was unsuccessful, but more would be heard from its sponsors; and Harp, too, were again in the throes of reorganisation with the familiar name of Diamond once more at the helm.

The new Dundee FC committee went about its business with great determination. Gilligan and Thomson went to Bolton, Longair and Burgess to Sunderland. Their replacements also came from across the border – most notably Kelso, a full-back from Everton who was later capped, and his team-mate Jack Hillman, a goalkeeper, and the first Englishman to move to a Scottish League club. The new season (1896–97) was viewed with great optimism and, captained by Kelso and inspired by Hillman, the new team once again made a good start. So much so, in fact, that the club decided to follow the example of others and become a limited company, thereby raising some much-needed capital for present debt and future investment. The *Sport* suggested a subscribed capital of £1,000 in £1 shares, with a £5 directorial qualification so that the 'working-class element' would not be eliminated from the management (again a change of tune); but in March 1897, when the first Dundee Athletic and Football Club Limited actually went on the market, 2,000 £1 shares went on offer. Unfortunately, the response from the public was poor, with only 500 shares being taken up. Thus only temporary respite was achieved by 'the Carolinas'.

Harp, too, had their problems. For one away game in Arbroath they only managed to raise three players and the prodigal Mr Diamond's efforts to have them registered by the SFA for various tournaments were invariably unsuccessful. But at least their expenses were minimal. Although fifth again in 1896–97, Dundee slipped to seventh place in 1897–98 and when they issued their balance sheet in March 1898 the extent of the difficulty was there for all to see. From an income of £3,265.2s.6d wages of £1,912.12s.8d. had been paid, and by the time other expenses such as guarantees were met, the club showed a net loss of £222.9s.2d. – even allowing for the new subscription of capital. In order to stave off the collapse which the close season would precipitate therefore, money had to be found, and indeed some local benefactors from the wine trade did come to the rescue. It was only temporary, however.

Once again players were transferred wholesale and the club

embarked upon season 1898–99 with a team which consisted
largely of part-time local players. Even the great Hillman fell
from grace. The big goalkeeper had been Dundee's most
popular player since his arrival and stories about him were
legion. Apparently his first landlady was a Gaelic speaker
whom he couldn't understand, and when she laid a plate of
porridge before him, he tackled it with a knife and fork! By the
beginning of season 1898–99, however, he was convinced he
was being retained as a piece of financial speculation and,
although he offered the club £100 for his own transfer (a large
sum of money for an individual to raise in those days), they
refused to budge. Hillman then took matters into his own hands
and began to 'play for his papers'. One day he pushed an
indirect free kick into his own net at Kilmarnock, thus giving
away a decisive goal. This, though, soon paled into insignificance when, in a derby match against the revived Wanderers,
he first disputed a penalty decision and then leaned against a
post as the kick was taken! Real 'tough-of-the-track' stuff and
club suspension followed. Hillman finally took his case to the
SFA meeting (from which he was eventually ejected) and later
he returned to Lancashire when Burnley paid £200 for his
transfer. A number of fans regretted the manner of his passing,
writing to newspapers in his defence. He was subsequently
capped by England.

Dundee's performances on the field, meanwhile, were
deteriorating rapidly. After 14 games they were bottom of
the First Division with three points, and at 11 a.m. on
Friday, 9 December 1898 they notified Celtic that their
game the following day would have to be abandoned. The
club, they said, was totally and irretrievably wrecked and
although the *Sport* complained that they should have
brought their shareholders together to give others a chance
to save the club, it recognised that the long record of
frustrated ambition could not go on and printed a short
epitaph: 'Thus ends an ill-starred venture.' (Ironically, the

epitaph would have been more suited to *Scottish Sport* itself, for while Dundee FC revived and looked forward to a long life, the *Sport* was to go to the wall some 16 months later.)

The following poem also appeared:

BURIAL OF DUNDEE
by 'No. XI'

1. Who killed Dundee?
   I, said the Celt
   My power he felt
   I killed Dundee.

2. Who saw him die?
   I, said the Ranger
   In his hour of danger
   I saw him die.

3. Who'll be the parson?
   I, said the Heart
   It's a big-line part
   I'll be the parson.

4. Who caught his blood?
   I, said the Clyde
   By the riverside
   I caught his blood.

5. Who'll mollify the Co?
   I, said the Hib
   With words so glib
   I'll mollify the Co.[3]

It was initially an intervention by the Scottish League which saved Dundee Football Club. At an emergency meeting on Wednesday, 14 December, the League offered to guarantee the club their expenses, including wages, in the four remaining league games. This was refused, the directors being 'sick of the whole affair' and having 'definitely decided to go into liquidation'. Also present at the same meeting, however, were two representatives of the earlier management, Mr Cameron and Mr Anderson. They were prepared to guarantee the continuance of the club under an enthusiastic and popular committee, given the League's offer. On 17 December 1898, Dundee Football and Athletic Club went into liquidation, but the idea of the new proprietors, said the *Sport*, was 'at once to strike terms with the liquidators, and so make the club *not a new body, but merely a reorganised continuation*, thus obviating the necessity of transfer of players and allowing business to be continued'. Also the word 'limited' was to be dropped from the name and the outgoing directors apparently went to unexpected lengths to ensure a smooth transference of business. When the new committee was elected (on 20 December) it contained a number of familiar names including those of Williamson, Cameron, Petrie and Shaw. So Dundee's wheel of fortune had come full circle. With the opening of Dens Park in 1899 (100 yards up the road from Clepington Park), and the re-establishment of the club as a limited company in 1900,[4] Dundee FC were ready to take their place at the centre stage of Scottish football. Some years later they would be joined on that stage by another great club.

NOTES

[1] Sandy Gilligan was the scorer of Dundee FC's first goal and the players received only 10s. per week initially.

[2] Dundee FC suffered the heaviest defeat in their history at Parkhead in 1895. With Longair concussed and off the field, they went down 11–0.

[3] The way people were feeling locally, 'mollicate' would have been a better word in verse five!

[4] The official Dundee FC programme (1983) lists 20 December 1898 as the date on which the present club was founded. This was indeed the date on which the committee which was ultimately to give the club continuity

was elected but, given that these same men had by and large been instrumental in founding the club in 1893, it is a date in the summer of that year which I believe should be the official one – either the date of the formal discussions between Our Boys and East End (20 May), the date of admission to the Scottish League (12 June), or the date of the election of the first Dundee committee (20 June). Furthermore, the new committee of 1898 was quoted at the time by the most reputable sports journal in the country, *Scottish Sport*, as wishing to make the club 'not a new body, but merely a reorganised continuation'. The directors of the Dundee Football Club at the turn of the century were: J. Robertson (chairman) (stair railer); A. Williamson (vice-chairman) (mechanic); G. Walker (machinist); A. Spalding (joiner); J. Cameron (collector). Shares were also held by D. MacLennan (traveller) and W. Wallace (clerk), who was also secretary/manager.

FIVE

If any discernible pattern can be said to exist in the city's footballing history, it is that when one team has been enjoying success, the other (or others, as it was in earlier days) has tended to suffer a relative decline. I am not suggesting that this is some kind of immutable law, that the future is fixed – indeed, I look forward to the time when the pattern is broken – but to date Dundee has never had more than one team enjoying success at any given time, although a case could be argued that if one club is enjoying major success this serves as a spur to the other to get down to some hard work and longer-term planning.

At the turn of the century, Dundee FC were shaping up for glory. Although Wanderers won the Northern League in 1899–1900, the Dark Blues[1] reigned supreme in the town, and when Dens Park was opened on 19 August 1899 they had an impressive stadium to match their First Division status.

The club appeared to have put their financial troubles behind them and under their first manager/secretary, William Wallace, proceeded to enjoy ten years of comparative success. In an 18-club First Division they were runners-up three times (1902–03, 1906–07 and 1908–09) on the third occasion losing the championship by only one point to Celtic and thus firmly establishing themselves as the most consistent 'provincial' club in the country. A number of their players were also capped by Scotland – William Muir, John Fraser, Peter Robertson, James Sharp, George Chaplin, Alex MacFarlane and John 'Sailor' Hunter. Sharp went on to play for Rangers, Fulham and Arsenal and has been described by the English press as 'a renowned defender of the Edwardian era', but it was Sailor – so called for his rolling gait – and his team-mates who would achieve immortality.

Remembering the better times with Jack Hillman, Dundee FC developed something of a partiality towards English League players and at least six of the 1909–10 team were brought to the club from England by Peter Allan, the scout who had earlier acquired the reputation of robbing local clubs of their best players. Herbert Dainty came from New Brighton; Jack Fraser and Alex MacFarlane from Newcastle United; Bert Lee from Southampton; Sailor Hunter from Portsmouth; and Johnny Bellamy from Woolwich Arsenal via Portsmouth. They, along with Crumley, Neal, MacEwan, Comrie and 'Puddin' Langlands, comprised the team which embarked upon the new season.

Their league performance was not quite up to the standard of the previous year, but a record crowd of 29,000 had attended a cup-tie with Rangers at Dens Park in 1909 and the 1910 campaign could not come quickly enough. In the first round the club drew minor opposition in the shape of Beith (away) but, as was the custom, the bigger club purchased the ground rights. It still took two games, however, both played at Dens Park (1–1, 1–0), to account for the Ayrshire men. In the second round Dundee were at home to Falkirk, who were second top of the First Division, but they were more easily dealt with (3–0); and before a record attendance at Fir Park, they dismissed Motherwell, by three goals to one.

In the semi-final, Dundee met the Edinburgh Hibs, a top-class team. It was not until the third game, played at Celtic Park, that they secured a 1–0 victory, with Hunter getting the winner (the first two games resulted in 0–0 draws) to take them to a final against Clyde. The Blues now genuinely believed they had a great chance, for Clyde had provided a remarkable series of shocks in the tournament, defeating Rangers, Queen's Park and Celtic in earlier rounds. With great anticipation, the Dundee fans made their way to Ibrox Park on 9 April 1910. In all, some 50,000 people attended this match and an outstanding game resulted in a 2–2 draw, Langlands, with the last kick of the match and Robertson (own goal) equalising two first-half goals by Clyde. This meant a replay and again the match was drawn, this time 0–0, but the *Daily Record* gave Dundee the 'artistic' edge in the second game. By the time the third game came around, the pendulum of favour was definitely swinging from west to east.

On Wednesday, 20 April 1910 the Scottish Cup came to the City of Dundee for the first (and, to date, the only) time. The famous team was: Crumley; Neal and MacEwan; Lee, Dainty and Comrie; Bellamy, Langlands, Hunter, MacFarlane and Fraser.

Chalmers opened the scoring for Clyde in three minutes, but the Clyde captain then made the tactical error of dropping back instead of pressing home the advantage; and when Bellamy equalised with a header before half-time, the Dundee hopes were high. In the second half it was their fitness which commentators believed gave the edge, for it had been a bad winter and all three games had been played in heavy conditions. It was therefore fitting that the training of former stalwart 'Plum' Longair should play its part in the club's first real moment of triumph. Late in the match, with some Dundee supporters having left early in anticipation of another draw, Hunter took advantage of a blunder by two

Clyde defenders and shot over the shoulder of the goalkeeper and into the net. 'Thus cups are won and lost,' said the *Record*.

Lee, Dainty and Fraser were the men of the moment, having performed superbly in all three games. An emotional Bailie Robertson, in accepting the trophy, could only find enough words to say that it was the height of the club's ambition to win the Scottish Cup. The team were cheered off by several thousand at Buchanan Street station; cheered again by large numbers at Perth; and when they arrived at the old West Station at eleven o'clock that night, between 15,000 and 20,000 people awaited them. Horses were taken from a brake (carriage) and all the players and officials were pulled in triumphant procession through the main streets,[2] The day culminated in supper at the Royal British Hotel. It was the early hours of the morning before the town quietened down. The players' bonus, it was thought, would reach 'double figures' (£10 or £15)[3] and with public subscription might rise to £30 – a lot of money when one considers that most agricultural labourers earned less than £1 a week at the time.

The press reaction locally, however, was somewhat muted the next day. Although the *Courier* reported that cheering crowds had fought for the special edition of the *Evening Telegraph* earlier in the night (something which can't have happened too often), its editorial was bland and extreme. And even the *Advertiser* – 109 years old and described on its centenary by the *Record* as having been a 'strong liberal organ when liberalism was unfashionable and its advocates propagators of sedition' – even the 'radical' *Advertiser* found space to bemoan the fact that the cup was 'won to a large extent by southerners'.

NOTES

1 Dark blue jerseys were not officially adopted by the club until 1902. From 1893–96 they alternated between the dark blue of Our Boys and the blue and white stripes of East End, and from 1896–1902 they played in what became the 'alternative' Dundee strip of white shirts and black shorts.

2 The brake actually collapsed in Victoria Road and the players had to complete the journey to Dens Park on foot.

3 Cup final teams:

First game: Crumley; Lawson and Chaplin; Lee, Dainty and Comrie; Bellamy, Langlands, Hunter, MacFarlane and Fraser.

Second game: Neal replaced Lawson.

Third game: MacEwan replaced Chaplin.

SIX

Dundee FC's Scottish Cup victory was rightly hailed as a fine achievement by everyone in football, but it was far from the case that all the other clubs in the town had given up hope of emulating their success. Certainly, Harp had lost the initiative by regularly going in and out of business, but Wanderers and the still-amateur Lochee United (the 'Queen's Park of the North') had both battled into the twentieth century and it was not only the Dundee patrons who were grateful for this. Many commentators remarked around the time that had it not been for the hard work of the officials of these clubs, not only the Forfarshire clubs but, also, those Aberdeen – Victoria United, Orion and Aberdeen – would have been isolated and in great difficulty. Perhaps recognising this fact, the three Aberdeen teams decided to follow the Dundee FC example and amalgamate as Aberdeen Football Club. In 1903 the new grouping took up residence at Pittodrie – a Celtic word meaning 'dung-heap'!

The Dundee soil, however, did not prove so fertile for Lochee United and Wanderers. By season 1907–08, both clubs were anchored at the foot of the Northern League, which by then had also incorporated some Fife teams, and following their deposition at St Margaret's Park by Harp Juniors,[1] Lochee United failed to compete in the 1908–09 league. A new ground was eventually found by the club (also in Lochee) but Wanderers were not so lucky.

Following another poor season (1908–09) their lease of Clepington Park became due. Now whether more money was offered is uncertain, but the Wanderers were suddenly shocked to learn that a Mr Pat Reilly, secretary of the newly formed Dundee Hibs, had approached the Clepington landlord over the heads of the Wanderers to secure the lease – and thereby evict them from the ground which had been their home, almost without interruption, for some 19 years. This proved to be a virtual death blow to the Wanderers, for although they managed to turn in some creditable performances over the next few years, particularly in view of the fact they had no permanent home, they never recovered the lost ground (so to speak) and went out of business at the onset of the First World War. Their magnificent efforts, however, in endeavouring to rival the more powerful Dundee amalgamation – and, even more important, in identifying and consolidating the Clepington area as the natural 'home of football' in the town – should not, and indeed did not, go unrecognised.

What was this organisation, the new Dundee Hibs, and where had they come from? The *People's Journal*, believe it or not, was at this time a fairly radical sister-paper to the *Dundee Advertiser* and, as such, in touch with the Irish community in the town. On 20 March 1909 it recorded the following:

> For some time there has been talk in the city with regard to the formation of a new Irish senior team and a committee, at the head of which is Mr P. Reilly, cycle dealer, is working at the business. Of course everyone wants to see a return of the days when the old Harp was a power in the land, but it is much to be feared our enthusiastic friends

scarcely know the magnitude of the task they have undertaken in these altered times. Meanwhile the plan is to secure a ground in the *east end*[2] of the city [my italics], one being in view, and also to seek admission to the Northern League, which should be easily gained in view of recent developments, for St Johnstone and Arbroath have decided to follow the Fife clubs into the new Central League. As to players, the committee is pleasingly optimistic, and friends of the game will wish them well in their endeavour to restore the lost prestige of Irish football in the city. It will be an uphill task but perseverance, enthusiasm and money, may accomplish much.[3]

Dundee Hibs, therefore, were founded sometime in the second half of March 1909. It was obviously not their original intention to dispossess the Wanderers of Clepington Park and when it was announced (on 17 April) that they had done so, it was not the morality but the wisdom of such a move which was questioned by the *Journal*. 'It is the proximity to Dens Park,' said their correspondent, 'which has been the undoing of the Wanderers who, if they can manage to get a ground in another quarter of the city will be well out of Clepington.' Or on 1 May: 'The Wanderers have got notice to quit so that the *nice little tangle* has got beyond controversy and the public knows how matters stand. The new Hibs mean to do big things and it is hoped they will be successful, but they have certainly made a very big initial blunder in going to Clepington Park *which has been a starvation hole from first to last*' (my italics).

A 'nice little tangle' it certainly was and, like the Harp before them, it was noted on Hibs' record by the footballing fraternity. The 'Forkies' were particularly embittered and although instructed by a lawyer to leave the fittings of Clepington Park, they ignored him and sold them to a 'wrecker', stipulating that he was to remove everything from the field. Hibs offered him £20 profit on his transaction to allow the erections to stand, but Wanderers would not listen and even removed the fence which, as Dundee FC player Sandy MacFarlane noted at the time, left Clepington Park 'bare as a bald head'.

Whatever their initial difficulties, however, Dundee Hibs, in keeping with their Glasgow counterparts, appear to have found a great enthusiast and legislator in Pat Reilly. Reilly (born 1874) had come from Ireland as a child with his parents and entered the cycle trade at the age of 18, opening a shop on the south side of Perth Road. The business prospered when women took up cycling and he then opened branches in Leith, Perth and Edinburgh, where he developed a keen interest in the fortunes of Edinburgh Hibs.

This association then fired him to establish a similar club in Dundee (a senior Irish club, Erin Rovers FC, was also established in Perth in 1909) and with the support of Tom Timmons, T. Malone, John Naulty, James Glover, J. Hennessy and ex-Provost Hawick of Forfar (Wallace the baker also had a financial interest), he founded the Dundee Hibs. Reilly was active in Liberal politics and church business but the new club, whilst acknowledging the importance of the Catholic Church in the community at large, appear to have decided not to have clergymen *directly* involved in the running of their affairs, and were never sectarian in their choice of players.

They played in green jerseys and white shorts and on Tuesday, 25 May 1909, were admitted to the SFA. The Dundee papers did not report this, in spite of the fact that the Hibs had been pressed by the SFA to produce evidence that they had indeed taken over the tenancy of Clepington Park, but on 1 June they did mention that at a meeting of the Scottish League the previous night, Dundee Hibs, by obtaining only three votes in a ballot, had failed to gain admission to the Second Division. The Hibs were undeterred, however, and on 18 August 1909, in front of 7,000 fans, they inaugurated Tannadice Park (which Clepington Park had been renamed) with a match against their Edinburgh namesakes. It was a gala occasion and memories of the old Harp were revived[4] when the Very Rev. Provost Holder congratulated the directors on their fine team. The band from the *Mars* training ship played and Dundee Hibs lined up: Brady (from Lochgelly United); Hannan (St Johnstone) and Gallacher (Wanderers); Strachan (St Joseph's), Ramsay (Brechin City) and Boland (St Joseph's); Flood (Dundee A), McDermott, Docherty (both Forfar), Dailly (Dundee A) and Brown (Kirkcaldy United). In a 1–1 draw, the Edinburgh Hibs player who scored the first goal of the match won a bicycle, and it was Docherty who equalised. The following week the wolf lay down with the lamb when the aggrieved Wanderers returned to Tannadice, but for once it was the lamb who knocked it off, Wanderers winning 2–1.

Dundee Hibs' first victory came on 28 August when, in front of a handsome gate, they defeated Montrose 1–0, although the first local derby between them and Dundee resulted in a 3–0 victory for the Dundee (A) team. The Hibs did much better in the next match (February 1910), however, when a narrow 1–2 defeat at the hands of the Scottish Cup heroes served to raise a few eyebrows in the town. The club was now determined to make its presence felt in any way possible. On 9 April they flew in the face of tradition by arranging an away game against St Mirren at Paisley when Dundee were playing their first Cup final seven miles along the road at Ibrox. With another piece of monumental opportunism they arranged to play Clyde at

Tannadice two days after the final! Reilly's tactics obviously worked, however, following some canvassing and the distribution of a circular in May 1910 in which he informed the other Scottish clubs that: the Hibs had spent £3,000 on Tannadice and were now clear of debt; the pavilion was two storeys high and built of brick; the dressing-rooms were fitted up in the latest style, with cold and hot water baths; the stand could take 1,200 people and the ground 15–20,000; and the club's inclusion in the Second Division would gratify the city's 50,000 Irish population and open up interest in that League. Following this public relations exercise he secured their admission to the Second Division on 7 June 1910.

Neither the Northern League nor the East Coast Carrie Cup was completed that year, but both tournaments gave the club useful experience and when Second Division football returned to Tannadice after almost 16 years, the Hibs were ready for it. The first two matches against Leith and East Stirling were lost, but a 4–1 victory over Abercorn on 17 September was followed by three draws and three wins and, following some heady days near the top of the league, they finished a creditable ninth in their first season.

Dundee FC, meanwhile, finished fourth in the First Division and gave a stout defence of the Cup, reaching the semi-final in which they lost 3–2 to Hamilton Accies – and the city also experienced the excitement of a General Election (December 1910) in which one of the MPs elected for Dundee was none other than Winston Churchill. A Liberal at this time, Churchill had first been elected to represent Dundee at a by-election in 1908 and confidently expected to hold the seat for the rest of his life. Dundee folk, however, are not as green as they're cabbage-looking.

The high-water mark in the history of Dundee Hibs was reached in season 1913–14. The Hibs were early exponents of a local scouting system and their first team, which by then included nine locals – a record for a First or Second Division club – was in with a chance of going into the First Division, as there was talk of increasing the number of clubs to 20 (there was no promotion at this time, but the club had had a good season).

Promotion did not, in fact, materialise, but the Hibs were not to be denied their moment of glory and it came in the Qualifying Cup. This was a lesser tournament than the Scottish Cup, obviously, but fiercely contested nevertheless by Second Division and other senior clubs. The early results were as follows: first round, Hibs 2, Brechin City 0; second round, Hibs 3, Dunfermline 0; third round, a bye; and fourth round, 2–1 at home to East Stirling, following a 1–1 away draw. The fifth-round game with Forfar at Tannadice was the 'talk of the town and country' and Reilly was indignant at suggestions that the club might ask for the use of Dens Park to accommodate the anticipated 15–20,000 crowd. In the event, Tannadice was improved for the game which was won 1–0. Hibs were now unbeaten for a year at home in League and Cup but they were taken to a replay in the semi-final by Inverness Caley. Five hundred fans made the journey and witnessed a 2–0 victory in the Highland capital.

On Saturday, 13 December 1913, they met Albion Rovers in the final at Tynecastle. The Dundee Hibs team was: McPhillips; Hannan and Forbes; White, Henderson and Boland; Brown, E. MacDonald, Martin, Linn and Stoessel. The first game was drawn 1–1 (Brown) and so was the second, 0–0 at Easter Road, and these were good performances from the Hibs team who lagged behind the Whifflet team in the League. On Saturday, 27 December, they returned to Tynecastle, only to lose 3–0, but, all things considered, the future was not looking altogether unpromising for the Tannadice Hibs when the nation received the news on 4 August 1914 that Britain was at war with Germany.

NOTES

1 Harp (seniors) collapsed in 1897 partly because they could not find a permanent home. Harp (juniors) began in 1904 and they, too, were without a home until they replaced Lochee United at St Margaret's Park (Gardner Street/ Kilberry Street) when they became known as Lochee Harp. They were therefore different clubs but from the same tradition, and their strips and club badges were identical.

2 The *Evening Telegraph* reported that the club had tried to find a ground in the west end. The *Catholic Herald* said two sites were under review.

3 The *Catholic Herald* (27 March 1909) also said: '. . . Dundee Hibernians are now a duly organised body . . . The promoters are all Dundee Irishmen, and as the city is said to include in its population no less than 30,000 of the same persuasion, the new organisation will not want support. Mr P. Reilly . . . has been appointed secretary. The new club is meant to take the place of the defunct Harp.'

4 Paddy Rock, formerly of Dundee Harp, hoisted the green flag over Tannadice at the inaugural game.

SEVEN

Although both Dundee FC and Dundee Hibs maintained teams throughout the First World War, football obviously became something of an irrelevance. The 'B' Division was suspended and at one point both Dundee FC and Aberdeen were asked to stand down from the First Division to minimise travelling. On the resumption of the First Division proper in 1919, however, Dundee FC, with former player Sandy MacFarlane installed as manager (Dundee's first full-time paid official), and William McIntosh as chairman, went on to build some of their best-ever sides. Although they did not win anything, they reached the final of the Scottish Cup in 1925 and contained a number of outstanding individuals. There was goalkeeper Willie Fotheringham; 'iron-men' Dyken Nicoll and Willie Rankine; David 'Napper' Thomson, a full-back who was capped against Wales; Davie Raitt, also a full-back and great character who was transferred to Everton in 1922 but later returned to the city; Davie Halliday, a prolific goalscorer who came originally from Dumfries and who held the club record until the 1940s (38 goals in one season); and Alec Troup, the first Dundee FC player to be capped against England and who would undoubtedly have received more honours but for the fact he played in the same left-wing position as the 'Wee Blue Devil', Alan Morton of Rangers. Troup was transferred to Everton in 1923.

The post-war Dundee FC management showed great enterprise in buying Dens Park in 1919 for £5,000 and by the time the ground had been renovated and a new grandstand built in 1921 (the one which remains today),[1] the club was said to have spent some £60,000. This meant a new issue of capital, but contrary to the expectations and desire of many of the supporters, the club decided to remain a private company with approximately 30 new shareholders joining the existing 20 or so and the directorial shareholding increased from 25 to 200.

Dundee Hibs were just as ambitious, but neither as rich nor as successful as their neighbours. In season 1919–20 they competed in and won the Eastern League with a side which contained a number of ex-Dundee players. The usual pool was J. Crumley (later transferred to Swansea), Mulholland, Henderson, D.S. Miller, Wilson, Herron, Hughes, Bradley, Gibson, Cargill, F. Murray and Wilkie, Pat Reilly remained in charge. In season 1920–21 the club moved into the Central League and improvements were made to the pavilion and dressing-rooms, but this was all in preparation for the return to the Second Division, to which they were admitted on its restart in 1921.

'We are on the eve of the greatest season in the club's history,' said one unnamed official and it was just as well he was unnamed, for his judgement was somewhat wide of the mark. In a disastrous season from a playing point of view, the club sank to second bottom of the league. Since 1921–22 was to be the first which led to automatic promotion and relegation, Dundee Hibs were dropped from the 'B' Division along with Clackmannan.

The year 1921–22 was a difficult time throughout Europe with post-war unemployment causing riots, and in Dundee the soup kitchen at Constable Street baths was serving up to 1,000 people per day. However, 1921–22 also marked a significant political development in Britain and one which was to conspire with the evil of unemployment to cast an even darker shadow over Tannadice – for this was the time of the Ulster Treaty, which, instigated by Lloyd George and supported by Winston Churchill, separated the six counties of Ulster from the 26 of the Irish Free State. Now, public opinion about Ireland had changed dramatically following the Easter Rebellion of 1916, and when the violence was stepped up in Britain after the war (indeed some Irish political prisoners were jailed at Perth) the position of a poor and lowly placed club with Irish connections would have become precarious indeed.

And it was not as though the local press handled the issue, or the clubs for that matter, with equanimity. Even allowing for the fact that Dundee FC were the more successful of the two, the Hibs' achievements prior to the war merited encouragement and considerably more than the occasional acknowledgement given to them by the so-called 'liberal' *Advertiser*. D.C. Thomson's *Courier* – whose leading sports writer went by the unambiguous pseudonym of 'Dark Blue' – devoted more space to the plight of Queen's Park, who faced automatic relegation to the Second Division, than to the plight of the Dundee Hibs, who faced extinction.

Fortunately, this bias was countered at an official level in the person of Willie Maley and when the Hibs announced their impending demise to the Scottish League on 28 June 1922, the club was assisted in the same way as Dundee FC had been in 1898. By what now might be called the 'Tayside Solution', players' registrations and transfer rights were held by the league to whom the clubs were requested to make offers, one third of which the league would retain. And as the Hibs also indicated a willingness to soldier on with a reconstructed board, a place was eventually found for them in the Alliance League which was the province of the reserve teams of First Division clubs.

In this new situation help was forthcoming from a number of sources, but none more unusual than the whimsically named UNOMI – football correspondent of the *People's Journal*. As stated above, the *Journal* remained fairly true to its historical liberal principles following John Leng's decision to bring his publications under D.C. Thomson's umbrella, and as late as the 1920s its football correspondent held a remarkably independent line.

First of all he welcomed the proposed reconstruction of the Hibs board. Reilly and his men had done a fine job and would retain an interest in the club, but a new challenge was now to be faced and the prospect of a new board of local businessmen buying out the old company and floating a new one seemed to UNOMI to be the correct path. The new chairman was James Dickson. His principal directors were William Hutchison, William Hogg, William Burke jun., and David Simpson. A club manager was also appointed in December 1922, one Peter O'Rourke, who had previously managed Bradford (although he lasted only four months).

At this point UNOMI entered the annals of the club's history. Following a first-round Scottish Cup Hibs victory over Beith, the journalist fell into conversation with some friends who, like himself, were puzzled as to why this reasonably attractive match should pull only some 3,000 people – one quarter of the attendance at Dens Park the same day where Dundee FC met the 'minnows', Vale of Atholl. What emerged from that conversation was of great significance to the Tannadice club, for in his next article (20 January 1932) UNOMI put forward the suggestion that Dundee Hibs change their name. 'No tradition attaches to the Dundee Hibs,' he said, except one, 'associated with misfortune'. Indeed, the name was 'a barrier which keeps many from giving personal practical support to the club' and, reading between the lines, there is no doubt that what everyone was talking about was the Irish connotations of the name. The article created a sensation in local football circles, or at least so UNOMI said, and his headline the next week ran, '*PEOPLE'S JOURNAL* TIP ADOPTED'. Underneath he revealed that the club were to take up his suggestion, keeping the name Dundee Hibs until after their application to rejoin the league was considered, then changing it to Dundee City.

By May 1923 the representation had been made and, at the expense of East Stirling, Hibs returned to the 'B' Division with Arbroath. It was later revealed that William McIntosh, the Dundee FC's influential representative on the league committee, had opposed Hibs' return on the grounds that he did not think the city of Dundee could maintain two 'First League' clubs. William Hutchison naturally disagreed and personally thanked the *People's Journal* for their support.

Not everyone, of course, was absorbed by the idiosyncrasies of football. At least in Dundee, Buffalo Bill was still alive. Well, actually, he was dead, but his memory and that of the Wild West lingered on, for in the summer of 1922 none other than 'Young Buffalo' (who?) was billed to appear at the King's Theatre (later the Gaumont Cinema and now the County Bingo). The show was apparently a 'romance' which featured 'real Red Indians' and a horse which a reviewer said 'could do everything but speak'. That made a change. (In the more credulous 1890s the *Advertiser* had carried a piece about a donkey in America which, it was reported, actually could speak!) On a more serious note, at this time Dundee's jute workers became embroiled in a strike which began in February 1923 and, in the case of the Lochee workers, lasted for 27 weeks, including two periods of lockout.

On 29 May 1923, Dundee Hibs appointed Jimmy Brownlie, the famous Third Lanark goalkeeper, player-manager of the club. Brownlie had won a number of caps for Scotland between 1909 and 1914 and his arrival marked the beginning of a new era in Dundee football. Alexander Lamb replaced Burke on the Hibs board and at an AGM on 20 August 1923 the club formally decided to change their name to Dundee City. The *Courier* had also predicted that the name would be changed, as 'the Irish element in the management of the club has practically been eliminated' and, although the choice of words was perhaps unfortunate, of the new board members only Simpson had any connection with the old Hibs club and he would last only until 1925 – all of which reinforces the belief that there was a definite move afoot to play down the 'Irishness' of the new club.

Applications were now put forward to the SFA and the Board of Trade in respect of the Dundee City Athletic Association. The Register of Joint Stock Companies finally sanctioned the Dundee City Athletic Club Ltd, but the letter to the SFA arrived only one day before their meeting on 19 September 1923 (shades of Dundee County, Harp and Dundonians). Once again Dundee FC protested, this time on the rather curious grounds that there was a possibility of 'confusion of correspondence'. Further, it was not in their (Dundee FC's) interest 'to have another club bearing the principal part of their name (Dundee) in such a similar title'. UNOMI immediately sprang to the defence of common sense, and of Hibs. 'I wonder,' he asked rhetorically, 'how the Sheffield clubs manage; also the two Manchester combines and the rival organisations of Bristol and Bradford?' UNOMI also criticised Dundee FC's delay in making their protest and, given that the Companies Register had passed the name, asked 'what price a legal argument?'

Dundee FC were simply 'getting the breeze up' remarked

one newspaper letter-writer, but following some discussion the casting vote of chairman T. White of Celtic went against Hibs' proposal. Two members of the SFA committee, however, whose votes would have given Hibs the change they sought had to leave early (one actually missed his train into the bargain) and so, on 17 October 1923, the Tannadice directors tried again. No comments were forthcoming at this meeting so the letter was allowed to lie on the table whilst the clubs conferred outside. There it was 'agreeably entertained that the name of Dundee Hibernians FC be changed to Dundee United'. Dundee FC were represented by McIntosh who apparently only objected to the name Dundee City, whilst the Hibs' men, Hutchison, Hogg and Brownlie, were willing to adopt any name 'so long as the word "Hibs" went out'. McIntosh then returned to the meeting and placed the proposal before the president, saying Dundee FC would support it.[2]

'The bond of friendship,' said the *Journal*, 'has been sealed between the clubs and nothing but harmony will prevail in future. In fact, there may be quite a lot of "come and go" between the respective officials and this, I think, should be for their mutual benefit.' Just how much 'come and go' would actually take place no one, least of all William McIntosh, could have foreseen.

In their first game as Dundee United, played against King's Park of Stirling on 20 October 1923, the Tannadice team beat the Second Division leaders by three goals to two[3] away from home. They lined up: Brownlie; Kay and Stirling; Swan, Richards and Porter; McEwan, Cottingham, O'Kane, Mackie and Gilmour; with Gilfeather as reserve. Their colours, white shirts and white shorts (the intended black shorts did not materialise for this game) earned them their first nickname, the 'Bakers'[4]

To summarise, therefore, Dundee United suffered a longer period of gestation than Dundee FC and in some ways it was a more complicated birth. Although not the result of an amalgamation in the final analysis, they were nevertheless the result of a fusion of ideals which ultimately could only prosper if the positive qualities of the Wanderers (a *friendly* 'Scottish' club with good staying power) were allied to those of the Hibs or Harp (at times *dynamic* 'Irish' organisations, due mainly to the personal commitment and drive of their best-known officials) in an organisation dedicated to good football of a non-sectarian character.

In many ways the appointment of Jimmy Brownlie – a respected professional and a Protestant – provided the link, almost in the same way that, many years later, a man with similar 'credentials' would galvanise another Scottish club with Irish connections.

NOTES

[1] The original grandstand brought from Carolina Port was on the opposite side of Dens Park and burned down in 1921. In his autobiography *Soccer Rebel*, Jimmy Guthrie hints at the insurance implications.

[2] The *Catholic Herald* by this time had apparently given up on the Hibs, as none of this was reported.

[3] United's goalscorers were Mackie (2) and Gilmour, Mackie scoring Dundee United's first.

[4] Dundee FC's first nickname was the 'Sugar Bags', as dark blue and white were the colours of the sugar bags made in the Dundee mills.

EIGHT

This, then, was the 'Roaring Twenties'. Jack Dempsey was heavyweight champion of the world; Rudyard Kipling replaced J.M. Barrie as Rector of St Andrews University; and at the General Election of 1923 Dundee once again returned the Prohibitionist, Neddy Scrymgeour, who had caused a sensation the previous year by ousting Winston Churchill as one of Dundee's two MPs.[1] No party was strong enough on its own to form a government but, with the support of the Liberals, the Labour Party came to power for the first time on 21 January 1924, and with Scot Ramsay MacDonald as Prime Minister.

The *Daily Record*'s election editorial had struck what was to become a familiar tabloid chord by exhorting the Liberals 'not to open the door to Labour extremists by rejecting a coalition with the Tories' and its sports pages also had a familiar ring. Dundee FC's failure to mount a serious challenge, it contended, could be attributed to the fact that the club's good scouting system was continually negated by a willingness to transfer good players. A successful United, it contended, would also help Dundee – although what would help United it did not say.

In season 1923–24 United finished ninth and Dundee FC fifth in their respective divisions, but 1924–25 was to be a better one for the clubs. United, who by this time had adopted the black and white colours, topped the Second Division after seven games and maintained an unbeaten away record until the end of November. Dundee's league form that season was not so convincing and on 24 December 1924, with the club lying twelfth, their manager, Sandy MacFarlane, resigned. The directors decided not to replace him right away but to look after the team themselves and it paid off to some extent, for in the Scottish Cup Dundee FC once again found form.

In the first round they defeated Johnstone 5–0 while United beat Aberdeen University 5–1. In the second round, the Tannadice team went down 5–1 to Partick Thistle (away) but Dundee beat Lochgelly United 2–1, and in the third round managed to account for the Cup-holders Airdrie, by three goals to one. In the fourth round Broxburn United were dispatched by one goal to nil at Dens, and in a semi-final replay, Hamilton Accies went the same way, by two goals to nil. United, meanwhile, were still enjoying *their* success in league football and continued to top the Second Division with the following side: Bridgeford; Kay and Osborne; Harvey, MacRoberts and Gilfeather; Simpson, Oswald, Collins, Bauld and Gilmour.

Dundee FC, however, had their sights on higher things and on 11 April 1925, in front of a 75,000 crowd, they met Celtic in the Scottish Cup final. Dundee FC lined up as follows: Britton; Brown and Thomson; Ross, W. Rankine and Irving;[2] Duncan, McLean, Halliday, J. Rankine and Gilmour. The Celtic team included two McStays, Patsy Gallacher and the young Jimmy McGrory, and the crowd was the second largest ever to have attended a Scottish Cup final. A number of special trains travelled from Dundee. Inside-right McLean (Davie, not Jim) opened the scoring for the Dark Blues after half an hour, and this was the only goal of the first half. In the 26th minute of the second half, though, something remarkable happened. Following a free kick, Patsy Gallacher collected and weaved towards the Dundee goal-line where the ball became lodged between his feet. Thinking quickly, instead of trying to release it, he simply 'rumbled over his wilkies' (no relation), thus throwing himself into the goal – and the history books. Four minutes from time, McGrory made it two and the Dundee support were forced to make that familiar and depressing journey home.

Davie Halliday, who had come to Dens via QOS and St Mirren, was soon after transferred to Sunderland (for £4,000) to replace the legendary Charlie Buchan, who was en route to Arsenal and his own magazine. Halliday was another who would have had more international recognition but for the excellence of the competition (Hughie Gallacher, McGrory), although he did get into the record books by scoring 100 goals in 101 games in the English First Division and in all scored 221 goals in 400 league and Cup games. His goalscoring equal would not be seen in a dark blue jersey for another 20 years.

On the same day as the 1925 Cup final, United secured promotion by beating East Stirling, and on 18 April they won the Second Division championship following a draw with Broxburn. Their record was: played 38, won 20, lost 8, drawn 10, goals for 58, against 44, points 50. Jimmy Brownlie's achievements were, therefore, quite remarkable in giving the city its second First Division club so soon and it was generally thought that when one or two positions were strengthened and fitness attained, United would develop into a good side.

On May Day 1925, Dundee City Athletic Club, formerly called Dundee Hibernian Football and Athletic Company Ltd, sold all 'business, property and assets, fixtures, fittings, erections and utensils' to the newly incorporated Dundee United Football Company Ltd. The price was 1,966 shares at £1 (which went mainly to the Reilly family) and payment of debts not exceeding £4,810.

In total, the Dundee United Football Company hoped to sell 2,500 shares at £1 but, initially, demand was slight. The directors, Hutchison, Dickson, Hogg, Lamb, Simpson and David Godfrey, pressed on regardless, buying Tannadice Park for £2,500 and issuing debentures of £4,050 at 5 per cent in cash with the ground used as security. The plan was that the whole income of the stand and half of the income of a projected new stand would be paid to the trustees in redemption of the debentures and interest. The Tannadice pitch was also to be levelled, drained and shifted west.

As was customary with a club entering the First Division for the first time, a league delegation headed by Willie Maley visited Tannadice and appeared to be favourably impressed by what they saw and heard. Once again, UNOMI was on the spot to record events for posterity and in a classic piece of journalistic enterprise he passed the following information on to his readers (30 May 1924): 'Prospectuses of the new company will be out next week. It is hoped the public will take an interest in the matter. *The officials want the club to be the People's club*' (my italics).

On 14 August 1925 United signed a strong, young forward named Jimmy Simpson[3] from Newburgh West End, and in their First Division match they lined up: Paterson; Kay and McBride; Campbell, D. Walker and J. Walker; T. Simpson, Bauld, J. Simpson, Howieson and J. McDonald. The match against Raith Rovers (away) was lost 4–2 (Howieson 2) but a victory was soon achieved against St Johnstone and on 19 September they astonished the Scottish footballing public by beating Celtic 1–0 at Tannadice to go above Dundee in the league. They then proceeded to slump badly, however, and after 11 games were in bottom position. The first First Division derby match was played at Dens Park on 21 November 1925. The score was 0–0 and United

71

were thought to have just as many fans as their neighbours. 'Plum' Longair described the result as 'a grand away result for United', but Glasgow's *Daily Record* continued in the traditional tone of patronisation. 'Jack is as good as his master,' said the columnist. United actually finished the season 17th with Dundee (now managed by ex-Celt Alec McNair) tenth out of 20.

And so the '20s roared on. The admission price for football was still sixpence and a crowd of 100,000 was recorded for an Old Firm match. Silent cinema was at its peak with Rudolph Valentino one of its great stars, although 'talkies' were on the way, and both would suffer competition from what was to become another pastime – popular dancing. Late-night dancing was in fact banned at this time in South Wales, where it was described by its detractors as 'dangerous excitement' and a 'sensuous menace'. Such over-reaction was probably due to concern about the general increase in social unrest which had developed in the so-called 'land fit for heroes' in the years following the First World War. Things came to a head on 3 May 1926 when a dispute between the National Union of Mineworkers and the coalowners (mines were in private hands at this time) escalated into a General Strike. The general action lasted less than two weeks, as the TUC had not been properly prepared for such a conflict, but the miners, faced with increased working hours or reduced wages, stayed out for some six months and individuals faced starvation in many cases. In Fife (and South Wales) their solidarity was particularly strong, but it was giving way elsewhere and following arbitration (by church bishops) they came to accept defeat.

In Dundee, the General Strike temporarily closed down both the *Advertiser* and the *Courier* and in a surprise development the heirs of John Leng, the distinguished proprietor of the *Advertiser*, transferred the controlling interest in that newspaper to David Couper Thomson, who had been his opposite number at the *Courier*.[4] The move was surprising because the *Courier* had been established in 1816 as the organ of Tory interest to combat the Liberal influence of the *Advertiser* (founded 1801) and Thomson had never shown the slightest sympathy for Liberalism. Having gained the effective press monopoly, however (for the Dundee businessmen who provided the essential advertising revenue had no interest in a Labour alternative – the *Dundee Free Press*), Thomson now relentlessly pursued an anti-trade union policy amongst his workers and was able to intensify the promotion of his parochial Tory viewpoint by virtue of the monopoly position. This would prove to be another factor in the shaping of the Dundee 'character'.

Dundee United began the year 1927 in 18th position out of 20 in the First Division, with Dundee fifth, but it was United who won the New Year derby match 1–0 with a last-gasp goal from right-back Jock Kay. Both clubs also had a good start in the Cup and a third-round tie with Celtic brought a record crowd (37,471) to Dens Park. Unfortunately, the match was lost 4–2 and United too went down in the next round, 5–0 to Partick Thistle. The Cup was eventually won by Celtic with John Thomson[5] in goal. In the final they defeated Second Division East Fife by three goals.

Cardiff City, meanwhile, with Sam Irving in their team, managed to win the FA Cup from the English Second Division and this would serve to give the Fifers continued heart. Alas, more than heart was required to save United, who were relegated, along with Morton.

NOTES

1 'What bloody shits the Dundeans must be,' said T.E. Lawrence (Lawrence of Arabia) on hearing of Churchill's demise. One wonders what he would have thought of that PLO flag in the City Chambers!

2 Sam Irving, a Northern Ireland cap.

3 Jimmy Simpson, father of Ronnie Simpson, later played two great games against Rangers and was transferred to Ibrox in 1927. He enjoyed a successful career there.

4 Leng himself had begun the process by amalgamating his *Evening Telegraph* with Thomson's *Evening Post* in 1905. The companies were effectively one entity from that date.

5 Thomson made his début for Celtic against Dundee at Dens Park in 1927.

NINE

The big football event of the late 1920s and early '30s was the Wembley Wizards' 5–1 thrashing of England in 1928; but the domestic game in Scotland at the time was dominated by a quality Rangers team under Bill Struth, with the main opposition coming from Motherwell, league champions in 1932 and managed by 'Sailor' Hunter, the former Dens Park favourite. A wave of spiritualism was reported to be passing over Dundee in 1927 but at Dens and Tannadice contact could scarcely be made with the living, such was the moribund state of both clubs. There was actually not a great deal to choose between the two at this time, but United would soon learn football's hardest lesson, that inconsistency can sometimes consign a club to a world far removed from that of its traditional rivals.

In spite of relegation, the Tannadice Terrors remained fairly buoyant and found their first 'star' player in Duncan Hutchison, a centre-forward and ex-miner[1] from Fife. 'Dunky' was just beginning to attract attention when United were drawn at home to Dundee in the second round of the Scottish Cup. He scored two in a match watched by more than 20,000 people. It was not quite enough, for although they were twice behind in the game, Dundee – augmented by two new English forwards, Whitlow and Lawley –

managed a 3–3 draw and won the replay 1–0. But revenge was not long in coming, for the next season, also in the third round of the Cup, the teams met at Dens Park. Hutchison was again the man of the match and although his early goal was equalised by Lawley, United won the replay 1–0. In the fourth round they were unlucky to draw Rangers at Ibrox but performed reasonably well before 50,000 people, going down 3–1.

The disappointment was short lived, however, for that season (1928–29) United won the Second Division championship again, with the following team: McGregor; Taylor and McLure; Dorward, Bain and Deuchar; Ross or Henderson, Hart, Hutchison, Kay and Michie or Cameron. Dundee FC finished third bottom of the First Division and escaped relegation by only three points, but the return of United to the upper bracket gave both clubs a shot in the arm and local rivalry once again intensified. Before the first derby match could take place (1929), however, the United fans were hit by a bombshell when it was revealed that their hero, Hutchison, for a fee of £4,000, was to team up with the legendary Hughie Gallacher in the colours of United's Newcastle namesakes. The fans were understandably most unhappy about this and when right-winger George Ross was later transferred to Portsmouth, chairman William Hutchison (no relation) was forced publicly to defend the club's policy. Whilst he recognised the fact that United were one of the best home-supported clubs in the provinces, he said, they would have 'gone bust' but for the money received for Hutchison and Ross. Whether or not this was strictly true will never be known, but the decisions were taken and the club prepared to accept the consequences.

Both derby matches were won by Dundee that season (1929–30) and the Dark Blues, now under Jimmy Bissett, were beginning to shape up as a good side. The half-back line in particular, of McNab, McCarthy and Thomson, was very sound and, although Thomson was later transferred to Everton, the fans were placated by the return of left-winger Alec Troup to his old stamping ground. Troup made his return début in the fourth-round Scottish Cup tie against Hearts at Dens and Dundee also signed a promising junior from Violet at this time – although it was in a different shade of blue that Scot Symon would eventually make his name. He came to Dens, however, in the face of stiff competition from other clubs and it was treasurer William McIntosh who received the credit. Unfortunately, such enterprise was not matched across the road and following a disastrous decline at the tail end of the season the Tannadice team were once again relegated.

Season 1930–31 was a better one for both teams. United went straight to the top of the Second Division, and by October Dundee were in second position to Celtic in the First. The fact that English clubs had imposed a ban on their Scottish players[2] in respect of playing for their country meant that a number of good home-based Scots got a chance, and left-back Jock Gilmour and right-half Colin McNab of Dundee FC both played for Scotland. Indeed, McNab was capped twice against England and in 1931 played his part in a 2–0 victory at Hampden.

Dundee's regular team at this time was Marsh; Brown and Gilmour; McNab, Symon and Blyth; Gavigan, Ritchie, Dempster, Campbell and Troup. In the second round of the Scottish Cup they beat Rangers 2–1 at Ibrox (Campbell and Robertson scored). Aberdeen, however, were their masters in the next round.[3]

United, meanwhile, scored a record 14–0 victory over Nithsdale Wanderers in the first round of the Cup and in the second round drew Celtic at Tannadice. The first match was postponed but the dream of a Tayside 'double' over the Old Firm narrowly failed to come true when United went down 3–2 (Kay and Bennett). The club, however, was holding its position in the league and a 2–1 victory over Dunfermline in the last game of the season at Tannadice was enough to give them promotion (1931).

The '30s was an era of great drama, upheaval and crisis throughout the world. At the beginning of the decade both Gandhi and Al Capone were in the news for breaking the law of their respective countries, although for different reasons. The great economic depression had led to rioting in cities everywhere, including Dundee, where the unemployed who marched against the iniquities of the means test[4] were baton-charged by the police and savagely sentenced for retaliation. And a floodtide of nationalism[5] began to sweep across the globe, carrying everything with it.

Even in Scottish football there was a tragedy when the unfortunate Sam English of Rangers, having been declared unfit earlier in the week, finally made the team and was involved in a clash with Celtic goalkeeper John Thomson. Thomson, who had been badly injured before as a result of his bravery, suffered a fractured skull in diving at the forward's feet and died later that night, 5 September 1931. Some 50,000 people attended his funeral at Cardenden in Fife, but the next day's newspapers suggested that events of a far more dramatic and sinister nature were about to engulf the world. For alongside the photograph of the Thomson mourners was one of a smiling Adolf Hitler. The leader of the German Nazi Party was pleased because the previous day, thousands of his followers had openly defied a police ban and worn their brown-shirt paramilitary uniforms at a rally in Gera.

The '30s also witnessed some of the most unusual behind-the-scenes activities in the City of Dundee's footballing history – events which had their origin at the inception of the Dundee United Football Club Ltd.

It will be remembered that the original company directors (May 1925) were William Hogg, a fruit broker;

William Hutchison, a wine and spirit merchant; James Dickson, a publican; Alexander Lamb, a newsagent and tobacconist; David Simpson, a manual teacher; and David Godfrey, a jute merchant (Jimmy Brownlie was company secretary). The number of shares sold, however, did not meet the anticipated figure and by October 1925 changes were afoot. First, David Simpson was replaced by David Halley (also a publican) and then a trust deed was signed in favour of William Hogg and William Hutchison who, by paying off certain debts at the bank, effectively took control of the club. Hogg and Hutchison then conveyed the assets of the club to themselves as trustees for the debenture holders. When Hogg died in 1927 he was replaced by local builder John Carnegie who, it was planned, would also receive payment for his work on the ground improvements from gate receipts. He now joined Hutchison and Halley on the United board.

That these men had the interests of Dundee United at heart was not in doubt, but the club was in financial difficulty from the start when its flotation failed to attract support and, as the position deteriorated in the late 1920s, the high ideals of the directors began to slip somewhat. No new stand was built and the gate receipts did not always find their way to the intended sources. This, Hutchison claimed later, was done out of financial necessity, as the gate-money was required to keep the club alive on a day-to-day basis (hence the Hutchison transfer in 1928). But such methods built up resentment on the board and matters came to a head following United's promotion in 1931.

By then, Hutchison, Halley and Andrew Boyd Carnegie (son of John, deceased) had a fellow director in Ernest S. Robertson (born 1892). Robertson's father had taken out 50 shares in the Dundee United Football Company in 1926 in the name of his firm, John Robertson and Son, aerated water manufacturers. On 1 December 1928 the company's shares were transferred to Ernest S. Robertson and on 8 March 1929 he became a director. Season 1930–31 had been a successful playing year culminating in promotion, but the club made a trading loss of £3,112.4s.2d. and its liabilities stood at more than £21,000. At a board meeting on 30 April 1931, Hutchison stepped down as chairman in favour of E.S. Robertson, and later Brownlie was replaced as manager by the ex-Rangers centre-forward, Willie Reid. The managerial job unfortunately proved too much for Reid and United were relegated again in 1932, the third time in five years. Although Hutchison was then replaced as a director, trading position also failed to improve, and for the year ending April 1933 United's auditors, Dickson, McIntyre and Co,[6] reported another substantial loss of £3,327.3s.8d.

At Dens Park there was also trouble in the boardroom and in this case it was William McIntosh who had become disaffected. McIntosh had begun his association with Dundee FC at the turn of the century and was to serve the game in an administrative capacity for more than 50 years. He became treasurer of the club in 1910, then a director in 1912, saw through the important structural changes at Dens in the early 1920s and took the club on its first European tour to Spain (1923–24). From 1927–33 he was also treasurer of the SFA and was personally credited with a number of outstanding signings for Dundee FC, including Troup, Cook and Symon. It was indirectly through his other great interest, however – music hall – that complications with the club arose.

McIntosh was proprietor of the Opera Bar in Gellatly Street which adjoined His Majesty's Theatre and Opera House (now the site of the ABC cinema) and was well known in music hall circles. When it came to social functions at Dundee FC, he was the obvious choice as supplier of refreshments and organiser of entertainment, but after one such occasion the club failed to pay his liquor bill and he sued (successfully) for the sum of £70.1s.3d. Relations with his fellow directors were, therefore, not very good and, sensing a wind of change at Dens (a new board under Wattie Simpson and a new manager, ex-Ranger Billy McCandless, had recently been appointed),[7] he first resigned as treasurer and then began to look elsewhere for a place to deploy his administrative talents. A turn of events at Tannadice soon gave him his opportunity.

United had begun the season 1933–34 calamitously, plunging to the bottom of the Second Division, and the debenture holders, their funds exhausted and repayable on 1 January 1935, now sought reconstruction of the company. A committee of debenture holders was appointed to confer with the directors and trustees and the prime mover on the committee was one Bailie George Greig, a wholesale tobacconist. The move came too late, for in February 1934, following a Cup exit and a league defeat by bottom club Edinburgh City, the situation was deemed so grave that United offered to resign from the Scottish League. Now 'certain parties',[8] it was revealed, had offered their assistance but did not want to disclose their scheme until league sanction was given to the club to withdraw its resignation. At a board meeting on Saturday, 24 February 1934, it was approved that these parties would in future control the team, although the directors would remain in office until the end of the season, when reconstruction would be considered.

The league then accepted a second United letter withdrawing the resignation. This paved the way for what most fans nowadays would regard as a bizarre situation of one man (William McIntosh) becoming a major shareholder of both Dundee United and Dundee FC simultaneously – a state of affairs which was to last for more than 20 years. What made things even more unusual was that McIntosh was one of the Dundee FC officials who opposed the return of Dundee Hibs to the Second Division in 1923, creating a certain amount of animosity between the clubs and their supporters in the process. Football, however, is a funny game and McIntosh now found himself at Tannadice.

On the playing side, Willie Reid 'resigned' and the old warhorse Jimmy Brownlie was reinstated as manager with ex-Dundee FC player Sam Irving as his assistant. Brownlie's first signing was also an ex-Dundee FC man, Andrew Campbell, and before the first Saturday match the players were taken for lunch to a local hotel where the first team of the new regime was announced. It was: McIntosh; Willis and Campbell; Corbett, Masson[9] and Lindsay; Ross, Brown, Auchterlonie, Gardner and Laing. Perhaps all they were really needing was a good feed, for they thrashed King's Park 8–1 (with five from Auchterlonie) and the following week beat Leith Athletic 5–2! The crowd (1,500) which turned up for the King's Park game, however, was quite disappointing and with Lochee Harp pulling 12,622 to a Scotland Junior Cup quarter-final that same month, the new United management obviously had its work cut out.

The new United board – Halley, Carnegie, Robertson, Greig, William Donald (a doctor) and John Millar (a hatter), constituted on 26 September 1935 – was responsible for at least one initiative which was to have far-reaching consequences for the club. The share capital was reduced from £25,000 to £2,500 divided into 25,000 shares of two shillings. The reduction of capital did not involve a diminution of liability and it meant that financial problems would continue to afflict the club, but what it did do was clear the way for a working-class directorate which would prove so valuable to United. The company ran into difficulty again in 1936 and George Greig, by lending them more money, became managing director with sole control. But even with the support of Robertson, he could not get the g|

club back onto a sound financial footing and in 1938 power
returned to the 'camp' of William Hutchison.

Hutchison, following a court case at the First Division of
the Court of Session in 1934, had resigned as a trustee but
remained a shareholder, and in 1938 rejoined the board
along with Donald, Brownlie, Carnegie and Irving. He later
transferred shares to Brownlie and Irving and his
directorship went to William McCutcheon (another
publican), but with Arthur Cram installed as company
secretary, the Robertson 'faction' once more gained control,
and with John Carnegie jun. adding the shares of the Reilly
family to those of his own (Pat Reilly died 1937) and James
Littlejohn replacing Sam Irving, the board took on a degree
of stability during the Second World War, which it has
maintained. William McIntosh was co-opted in 1945 and
Ernest Robertson became chairman in 1948.

NOTES

1 Dundee FC had their own star players at that time. Inside-left George
Gibson and left-winger Willie Cook were later transferred to Bolton
Wanderers and formed the left-wing of the Wanderers' side which won
the FA Cup in 1929. Cook was also capped.

2 Scots utterly dominated English football at this time. Jackson, James,
Gallacher and Morton were all in their prime and in 1928 Newcastle
United fielded a team against Leeds United in which only one player was
not Scottish born.

3 Again, Jimmy Guthrie's autobiography reveals that Dundee's trainer in the
early 1930s was an evangelist, Jack Brown. His favourite ploy was
apparently to set Protestants against Catholics in training, but when
tensions led to the postponement of a trial match, he was dismissed.

4 In Dundee in 1932 the number of married women refused benefit was 100
times that of Burnley, an English town half the size of Dundee.

5 Britain went for a National Government in 1929 when a General Election

failed to produce a clear majority for the Labour Party. Against the wishes of many in his party, Ramsay MacDonald went over to the grouping of National Unionists, National Liberals and National Labourites. In 1931 they won a landslide victory in the General Election, greatly reducing Labour's representation and utterly routing Lloyd George's Liberals. Michael Foot's brother, Dingle, was elected as a National Liberal and Francis Horsburgh, as a National Unionist (the only Unionist ever to be elected by Dundee), defeating Neddy Scrymgeour in the process; but as the '30s progressed, this 'National' grouping with first Baldwin then Chamberlain as Prime Minister, became generally seen as a 'front' for the Tory Party. In Dundee, for example, in 1931, local secondary school teachers were given a pay *cut* of 8 per cent. The National Government then stopped the town's Education Grant of £2,500, which meant that the cut would have to be *increased* to 10 per cent, and school fees at Harris, Morgan and Grove Academies and Lawside Secondary School also increased. Presumably those who could afford to pay the fees (£2–£5 per year) were not on the breadline.

6 In November 1933 this company took in as a partner a young accountant, James B. Gellatly.

7 Long-standing board members P. Jackson, A. McBain and W. McIntosh were replaced by J.W.A. Simpson, D.P. How, J. Ford and F. Graham. Simpson, How and Graham were jute merchants and the first-named reputedly a millionaire. J.W.A. Simpson, F. Graham, D.P. How and J.A. Galloway had made their money in the Indian jute trade. The first three acquired their substantial shareholdings in the 1920s when Dundee FC shares were undersubscribed and money was needed to pay for the reconstruction of Dens Park; Galloway came in in 1936 in place of John Ford. They gained control of the club in the '30s, ousting the 'old guard' of McIntosh, Jackson and McBain, and their methods of management were severely criticised by Jimmy Guthrie who, as a first-team player, was faced with proposed wage cuts on occasion. The unlikely name of Sir William Lamond, c/o the Imperial Bank of India, 25 Broad Street, London, EC2 also appears on Dundee FC's list of shareholders at this

time. His 75 shares were later sold to James R. Gellatly.

8 William McIntosh and George Greig among others.

9 Bill Masson, who also played for Dundee FC and became a director of physical education in the town.

TEN

The mid-1930s were a boom period for sports-mad Dundonians. As well as being 'fitba daft', Dundee was always a great boxing town and the fairground booths threw up some great local fighters like Freddie Tennant, who actually beat the up-and-coming Benny Lynch on one occasion.

Dundee FC opened the 1934–35 season with a victory against Rangers and were congratulated in the official United programme the following week. Both teams were in the top ten of their respective divisions and Dundee FC were getting particularly good service from their new inside-right or right-half Eric (Jimmy) Guthrie. United, meanwhile, signed a promising junior centre-forward called Arthur Milne from Brechin Vics.

In the league, the Dundee teams finished a creditable eighth and fourth in First and Second Divisions, but in the 1935 Scottish Cup, Dundee FC went out 2–1 to Motherwell in the first round. United, however, made a promising start by beating Fraserburgh 6–2 (away) in the first round, and Queen's Park 6–3 (home) in the second (with Milne beating Queen's Park goalie Desmond White four times). George Ross had returned to United (he would later be followed by his old ally Hutchison) and in the third round they drew 2–2 with Hearts at Tynecastle. For the replay at Tannadice,

Jimmy Brownlie planned to have an unemployed gate, but the idea was vetoed by Hearts and – in an incident which again reflects the dire poverty in which some Dundee folk lived – a crowd of around 300 people demonstrated at Tay Bridge station when the Hearts team arrived. The Jammy Tarts won 4–2 after extra time. Rangers eventually won that Cup, and Celtic the League.

In March 1935 Scot Symon asked for a transfer and in the 1935–36 close season he was signed along with Lew Morgan by Portsmouth, a club which was becoming something of a Scots colony at the time. (Guthrie would also join their ranks in 1937.) That and the latest local scandal kept the town gossip going. Dundee Labour councillor John Fraser, following the resignation of Chief Constable John MacDonald, asked the Scottish Secretary of State to initiate an inquiry into the behaviour of Dundee police force over the previous five years (MacDonald had lost a £3,000 slander action brought against a Dundee citizen).

The league performances of both clubs were again undistinguished, but in the 1936 Cup both did reasonably well. In the first round, Dundee FC beat amateurs Babcock and Wilcox 6–0 at Dens and United drew 2–2 with Alloa at Tannadice. The United replay was drawn 1–1 and United finally did the business at Tynecastle Park, but the most interesting feature of these games was that the Alloa team contained a fine right-winger called Bill Shankly (whose brother Bob was centre-half for Falkirk) and a strong full-back named Jerry Kerr! Both were promising youngsters at the time and both later progressed – Shankly to Carlisle and Preston and Kerr to Rangers, Edinburgh St Bernards and Hibs. In the third round Dundee beat Airdrie 2–1, while United went down 5–3 to Cowdenbeath, but in the fourth round, the Dark Blues crashed out 4–0 to Kilmarnock.

The local game, therefore, was in something of the

doldrums. But a Scotland–Wales international brightened things up at Dens Park in December 1936 and United fans were once again kept entertained by boardroom machinations at Tannadice. Following a very poor start to season 1936–37, Bailie Greig, who had resigned from the board some time previously, was suddenly called to attend a board meeting. It was later announced that he would assume 'complete control'. His keen business instinct was thought to have been missed and he immediately sought to get a good price for the in-demand Arthur Milne. 'I'm convinced,' he was quoted as saying, 'Tannadice has immense potentialities – and it's going to be my job to capitalise them.'

But national issues dominated the news. King Edward VIII was forced to abdicate in favour of his brother George, as 'morganatic marriage' – to a commoner (and divorcee) – was not possible under British law; 149,407 people (including 50,000 Englishmen) baptised the new Hampden Park; and in the Spanish Civil War German planes (assisting Franco) bombed the holy Basque city of Guernica, the first air raid on a civilian target. The world had changed, and the game of football had changed in the 1920s and 1930s too, with the offside and penalty rules being upgraded to their current status.

In Dundee it was now Dens Park which was the subject of rumour concerning behind-the-scenes moves. The net result of this was that Billy McCandless 'resigned' as manager, to be replaced by another ex-Ranger, Andy Cunningham ('Brainy, breezy and bowler-hatted,' said the *Record*; Cunningham was later a noted sports journalist.) Arthur Milne, meanwhile, went on trial with Liverpool but the option was not taken up and he then signed for Hibs, with whom he enjoyed considerable success.1 Dundee FC finished ninth in the First Division and United 14th in the Second.

Season 1937–38 began calamitously for United, who went down 7–1 at home to St Bernards. But as so often happens, a change at the top can breathe new life, and Dundee FC started brilliantly, with their team lining up: Marsh; Cowie and Rennie; Laurie, Evans and Smith; Regan, Baxter, Coats, McMenemy and Kirby. (Harry) McMenemy and Regan had been brought north from England at the time Charles Atlas was making his first appearances in the advertising columns offering to convert 'YOU!' from a seven-stone weakling to a champion; and Dundee began the season with seven straight victories, establishing a three-point lead at the top of the First Division.

Rangers, of course, were never far behind and the west coast press was in its usual state of admiration. Pictures, for example, would show 'Dougie' Gray of Rangers beating 'Warren' of Hearts to the ball. The Light Blues, however, did find a new goalscoring star that season – a young centre-forward called Willie Thornton – while at Parkhead a true goalscoring 'great' departed. Jimmy McGrory, who had scored 550 goals in 15 seasons, left to become manager of Kilmarnock.

Sadly, Dundee FC could not keep up their fine form. First, they began to slide from the upper reaches of the league and then they went out of the Cup in the first round, 4–2 to Albion Rovers. United, conversely, had found their form and they provided the big shock in that round of the Cup by defeating Hearts 3–1 at Tannadice, with their team: Nicholson; Collington and Grieve; Skelligan, Watson and Yorke; Duncan Hutchison, Clarkson, Rumbles, Robertson and Adamson. In the second round, however, they had the misfortune to run into the most famous East Fife team of all time, who beat them 5–0 at Methil, then went on to win the Scottish Cup (the first and only Second Division team to do so).

Things were now pretty bleak in Dundee. United were

not in the promotion hunt, both teams were out of the Cup, and in spite of a 6–1 victory over Rangers at Dens, Dundee FC had, unbelievably, slipped into the relegation zone of the First Division. On 30 April 1938, their fate was sealed when, with 31 points from 37 games, they drew the final match 0–0 (away) to Ayr United. The same day, Queen of the South beat Rangers 3–2 at Ibrox, so Dundee FC, a club reputed to have the richest directorate in Scotland at the time, were down along with Morton. No fewer than six clubs finished one point above them. United fans were equally despondent, for their favourites finished fifth bottom of the Second Division.

By the time the 1938–39 season got under way people were even *more* pessimistic, but now it was the prospect of war which alarmed them. One quarter of the world was already at war, Hitler, Mussolini and Franco were advancing, virtually unchecked by other nations, and photographs of air-raid shelters and gas masks began to make their rather ominous appearance in newspapers.

United won the first Second Division derby 3–0 at Tannadice (with English newcomer Horace Wooley scoring twice) two weeks before Neville Chamberlain returned from Munich with his famous 'piece of paper' which promised 'Peace in our Time'. Rangers signed Scot Symon from Portsmouth, who then proceeded to win the 1939 FA Cup with Jimmy Guthrie as captain. And Willie Cook returned to Dens Park and helped Dundee FC first to reverse the earlier derby result and then to attain sixth place in the Second Division (United finished ninth).

By then, however, Madrid had fallen to Franco's Falangists and when it was announced on 21 August 1939 that Stalin had signed a non-aggression pact with the Nazis, people were prepared for the worst. Children were evacuated (in Dundee's case many went to Kincardineshire), Britain reaffirmed its pledge of support to the now-exposed Poland, and when Germany attacked that eternal political whipping-boy on 1 September 1939, Britain and France responded with a declaration of war.

It was hard lines. Dundee were top of the Second Division and United second equal.

NOTES

1 Milne returned to United during wartime. His signing for Hibs cost United money because they had turned down £3,000 from Chelsea in favour of Liverpool's bid. When Liverpool failed to take up their option, Milne was not re-transferred to United and Hibs picked him up. United eventually got £750 after a complaint to the League.

ELEVEN

Dundee competed in the East and North East League for one season, then went into retirement until 1944. United, however, with Arthur Cram CA, as club secretary, carried on and played throughout the war with the exception of season 1940–41, a move which proved popular among local fans and helped to consolidate further their support. United also competed in the North East League but their real moment of glory was enjoyed in the 1939–40 War Cup.

In the first round, played on a home-and-away basis, they defeated Partick Thistle 4–2 at Tannadice and drew 1–1 at Firhill. In the second round an Arthur Milne hat-trick was the feature of a 7–1 victory over Third Lanark, Dundee's conquerors in the first round; and in the third, also played at Tannadice, they crushed Kilmarnock 3–0.

Guest players were allowed during wartime and once again the name of Jasper (Jerry) Kerr, now of Hibs, crossed United's path. Kerr played four games at left-back before injury necessitated his replacement by Tommy Dunsmore, also of Hibs, though, in all, only 13 players were used in the campaign. In the semi-final United met Airdrie and, following a 0–0 draw at Easter Road, the Lanarkshire team introduced none other than Stanley Matthews to their side. The great man, however, was played out of the game by

Dunsmore and the Terrors marched on to the final with a 3–1 victory.

This final match was played against Rangers at Hampden on 4 May 1940, and the attendance of 71,000 reflected the wartime hunger which existed for the game in Scotland. United lined up: Thomson; Miller and Dunsmore; Baxter, Littlejohn and Robertson; Glen, Gardner, Milne, Adamson and Fraser. Since the club was managerless (an ex-Morton and Rangers player, Robert McKay,[1] had come and gone with the onset of war), a Lochee businessman named Jimmy Allan helped look after the team.[2] Inside-left Adamson had the ball in the net in the first half, but the 'score' was disallowed and an inevitable goal from Rangers' Smith sent the Tannadice men home empty-handed. It had been a great effort, though.

After the war the ubiquitous William McIntosh and James Littlejohn, the wartime centre-half, joined Ernest Robertson, J. Carnegie, Arthur Cram and chairman W. McCutcheon on the United board. The appointment of Mr Littlejohn was particularly significant, as it reinforced United's policy of having ex-top-class players not only in the manager's chair but actually *on the board*. Jimmy Brownlie and Sam Irving, for example, were pre-war directors, Duncan Hutchison would later follow suit and eventually become chairman of the board, and Littlejohn's association carried on into the 1980s.

Dundee FC, by comparison, still tended to go for directors who were *primarily* substantial businessmen and one cannot but reflect that such a policy, inasmuch as it has continued, has not had a wholly beneficial effect upon the club in the longer term. In the immediate post-war period, however, it was the Dundee FC board which got its equation right and it was a former player who proved to be the crucial factor.

It is difficult to overestimate the contribution George

Anderson made to Dundee Football Club, but if any one man can be said to have consolidated their position as a leading provincial club and to have firmly established their reputation as, traditionally, a good footballing side, then Anderson was the man. An Aberdonian by birth, he had played in goal for Aberdeen FC and later served as a director at that club, but he also turned out for Dundee FC during the First World War and it was in their temporary demise that he saw his opportunity. In 1944 he built a new board around himself and together they faced the 'new' world.

In 1943 the war hero Churchill had been offered the freedom of Dundee, which he declined, but in 1945 it was once again his turn to be rejected, this time by the people of Britain in a General Election. The city elected two political inside-lefts – John Strachey and Tom Cook – in a Labour landslide and now prepared for a period of reconstruction and relative prosperity as new and more diversified industry was brought to the town.

United also had a new manager in Willie McFadyen, the ex-Motherwell star, but it was Anderson – 'Toffee Dod',[3] as the players called him – who continually made the running. Right from the start he showed himself to be a progressive football thinker, emphasising ball-work in training and psychology in man-management and public relations, and in the early '50s he actually called for a smaller, premier-style Super League on a number of occasions. Of course, it is often said that football is about players, but in this department Anderson also had a good eye. Doug Cowie, a young half-back from Aberdeen St Clements, was picked up in the face of stiff competition; Tommy Gallacher (son of Patsy), who had guested during the war, joined the club on a permanent basis from Queen's Park; Reg Smith, a skilful Englishman, who had also guested, came from Millwall; and no less an authority than Matt Busby commented publicly on the club's cultured style of play. Both Dundee and Dundee United were in the Scottish League 'B' Division in season 1945–46, but at the turn of the year Dundee were top and United bottom and in the January derby Dundee won 3–2 at Tannadice (recently stepped with railway sleepers).

Dundee FC actually topped the North East League in 1944–45 and the 'B' Division in 1945–46, but it was not until the conclusion of their third season of 'supremacy' that league reconstruction allowed them to progress to the 'A' Division. By this time another wartime-guest-made-permanent, Sammy Cox, had gone to Rangers to be replaced by Alf Boyd from St Johnstone, and a strong unorthodox centre-forward, Albert Juliussen, had written his unusual name in the history books. At two consecutive games in March 1947, Juliussen scored double hat-tricks, the first at Alloa in a 10–0 victory and the second (seven goals, actually) against Dunfermline at Dens, where the same score was registered. The double figures in successive games was also a record and Dundee FC were definitely now giving notice that as a club they were coming on-stream. Rangers won the 'A' Division that season (1946–47); Aberdeen (managed by Davie Halliday) took the Scottish Cup for the first time; and two new stars appeared in a Scottish jersey – inside-forward Billy Steel of Morton and Gordon Smith of Hibs, a right-winger who had been signed from Dundee North End.

At the beginning of 1948, Dundee lay fourth in a First Division of 16 teams and United twelfth out of 16 in the Second Division but United still had ambitions which were regularly aired in public and it should also be remembered that a number of clubs with a distinguished history (e.g. St Bernards) had failed to survive the wartime break. United also maintained their reputation for finding new talent, and forwards in particular. Outside-left George 'Piper' MacKay was swapped for Dundee centre-half Jim Dickson and, ironically, it was Dickson who did particularly well in the Tannadice defence, although they did lose five goals to Birmingham City in a friendly (the Birmingham players and officials were later presented with Timex watches, one of the new local products of which Dundonians were understandably proud). MacKay was followed into the United forward line meanwhile by his namesake, centre-forward Peter MacKay, but even his considerable goalscoring talents[4] could not raise the club from its lowly position. Rangers were also struggling to find form in the 'A' Division and the *Courier* managed to get in on the 'What's wrong at Ibrox?' act. Whatever was wrong at Ibrox, the 1947–48 League went to Hugh Shaw's brilliant Hibs side – the first time a provincial club had taken the title since Motherwell in 1932 – and this victory heralded the greatest years in the Edinburgh club's history, 'Famous Five' Smith, Johnstone, Reilly, Turnbull, Ormond, *et al.*

Dundee FC were also entering their most consistent period to date and the fourth position in the 1947–48 league was a foretaste of things to come. Again Anderson's foresight was in evidence for, following public statements that star players were not for sale and that young talent would be encouraged, the club proceeded to do just that. Out of the 32 players on the books at the beginning of the 1948–49 season, 20 had come from juvenile or junior ranks; and from eight who had come from local clubs, six were in the first team which went into the New Year in third top place.

The Dens Parkers were therefore attracting all the attention on Tayside, but things suddenly changed on 22 January 1949, when United played Celtic at Tannadice in the first round of the Scottish Cup. The game attracted 25,000 people and afterwards was described as 'the greatest Cup tie ever seen in Dundee'. United tackled the Celts with great enthusiasm and in all had the ball in the Bhoys' net seven times, although only four counted. United took the lead, then went two ahead before Celtic pulled them back. United then went ahead again, and again the Celts equalised before the Terrors grabbed the winner. I think it was around this time that the saying 'Dens Park for skills, Tannadice for thrills' originated and the United heroes on this occasion were: Edmiston; Berrie and Jardine; Ogilvie, Ross and Grant; Quinn, Dickson, MacKay, Mitchell and Cruickshank. Right-winger Frank Quinn, himself an ex-Celt, was one of the big stars of the United side and the scorers were Peter MacKay (2), Dickson and Cruickshank.[5] Unfortunately, the next round saw them in considerably less devastating form and the team lost 3–1 at Tannadice following a 1–1 away draw with Dumbarton.

Dundee FC meanwhile had the First Division's leading goalscorer in centre-forward Alec Stott; lay in second place to the Hibs in 'A' Division; and progressed to the semi-final of the Cup, where they lost 2–1 to Clyde. By the time that game had taken place, however, they had secured a 4–3 victory over the Hibs and sat on top of the league until the last game, which they had to win at Falkirk to become champions for the first time. Dundee's team was: Lynch; Follon and Irvine; Gallacher, Cowie and Boyd; Gunn, Patillo, Stott, Gerrie and Hill. In the first half Stott missed a penalty when Hill was brought down, and the Falkirk goalkeeper followed this up with a wonder save from Gerrie. It was not to be the Dark Blues' day, obviously, and in the second half Falkirk scored four times with one reply from Dundee. Tommy Gallacher later blamed the defeat on an uncharacteristic error of judgement by George Adamson, who locked himself and the team in the dressing-room for an hour before kick-off, thus unnerving the players. The team had not yet peaked, however, and with James Gellatly installed as chairman and Anderson as managing director, they looked likely to come again.

In 1949 Anderson signed a brilliant young goalkeeper from Carnoustie Panmure, the lanky Bill Brown, and he made his début for the reserve team on 10 October against Raith Rovers. A Canadian, Jack Cowan, and two South Africans, Gordon Frew and Ken Ziesing, were then fixed up; and on 21 September 1950 Anderson pulled off what was generally hailed as the transfer coup of the century when he paid Derby County £17,500 for one of Scotland's greatest-ever inside-forwards, Billy Steel.

Steel's transfer was indeed a bold move, but also a wise one in that whereas Dundee's defence was settled, the attack was not, and Steel provided the craft to bring out the best in the front line. His own career was fairly turbulent, ending in dispute both at Derby and Dens, and he was the first Scotland player to be ordered off. But his talent was undeniable and his début for Dundee on 23 September was watched by 34,000 people. Also, with admission prices ranging from 1s. 6d. for the ground to 5s. for the centre stand, he chalked £4,000 off his transfer fee straight away. As the *Courier* reported, all this fitted nicely into Anderson's 'master plan'. In the game, Dundee beat Aberdeen 2–0 and by New Year 1951 they topped the First Division with United in second place in the Second Division. Arguments about the respective merits of the two teams were also (temporarily) settled later that month when they were drawn against each other in the Scottish Cup and United fans must have thought they had it in the bag when they got a 1–1 draw at Dens. In an otherwise fine game, however, the United goalkeeper Wylie blundered once and Dundee FC scraped a 1–0 victory in the replay. Raith Rovers finally put Dundee FC out in the fourth round, but both Dundee and United maintained their league challenge and finished third and fourth in their respective divisions.

At Dens Park, though, not everyone was pleased with the way things were going and in April 1951, ex-Bailie John

Thomson, a former chairman of the club, resigned from the board of directors in protest at what he saw as George Anderson having too much of a free hand. But Anderson's policies were to be vindicated the following season.

In the League Cup Section C, Dundee faced stiff opposition from Hearts, Raith Rovers and St Mirren, but they qualified with a last-gasp victory at Starks Park. In the quarter-final they faced Falkirk – now in the Second Division, but the only unbeaten side in the country – and the Taysiders got through by drawing 0–0 at Brockville and winning 2–1 at Dens. In the semi-final Celtic and Rangers, who so often seemed to avoid each other on such occasions, were paired together (the game was won by Rangers) and Dundee booked their ticket to Hampden with a 5–1 victory over Motherwell.

On 22 October 1951, Dundee FC faced Rangers with the following side: Brown; Follon and Cowan; Gallacher, Cowie and Boyd; Toner, Patillo, Flavell,[6] Steel and Christie. Rangers scored first through Findlay, but any thoughts that this might finish it were dispelled when Flavell equalised early in the second half. In the 69th minute, 37-year-old Johnny 'Straight-Back' Patillo put Dundee ahead with another fine shot, but Rangers equalised when a George Young free kick could only be parried into the net by Brown. The Dundee players claimed that the goalkeeper had been fouled by Willie Thornton, but to no avail, and the match went into extra time. With less than a minute to go, Dundee got a free kick at the corner of the box on the South Stand side. Steel – who was later described as the real architect of the victory – floated it to the far post and there was skipper Alfie Boyd to head the ball into the net. Six thousand Dundee fans savoured their first real moment of glory for more than 40 years (attendance: 92,325).

George Anderson praised the coaching of Reggie Smith and the training of Reuben Bennett, and he described the result as a dream come true. Once again the train was met by thousands of fans at the station – by a strange coincidence the Dundee West railway policeman, James Goldie of Lochee, had also officiated 41 years earlier when the Scottish Cup came home – and the players struggled to Yeaman Shore where a bus took them for a triumphant drive through the town centre and then on to chairman Gellatly's house for a champagne party.

This was a good time for the city. Morgan Academy pupils won Radio Top of the Form (television was now also on the way); Frankie Quinn was selected for Scotland's 'B' team; and that same season (1951–52) Dundee reached the Scottish Cup final – although Motherwell's tactics of blotting out Steel paid off and they handed out a 4–0 defeat. In this game Bobby Henderson replaced Brown in goal (debarred by RAF duties) and George 'Pud' Hill was on the right-wing in place of Jimmy Toner. But disappointment soon turned to joy when, the following season, the club went once again to the final of the League Cup, where they met 'B' Division Kilmarnock who had defeated Rangers in the semi. Dundee FC's team was: R. Henderson; Follon and Frew; Ziesing, Boyd and Cowie; Toner, A. Henderson,[7] Flavell, Steel and Christie.

Manager George Anderson was taken ill before the game and a commentary was relayed to him at an Aberdeen nursing home. Reg Smith was a capable deputy, however, and two goals in the last ten minutes from Flavell gave Dundee a hard-fought victory (attendance: 51,830). Dundee FC were the first club to win the League Cup in successive years and if anyone had thought up the term 'New Firm' in those days then they and Hibs would have been the obvious candidates.

NOTES

1 McKay only lasted for two months, but in that time it was he who fixed up Jerry Kerr.

2 Ex-Dundee FC player later assisted Cram in the United camp.

3 R.S. McColl, founder of the High Street sweetshop chain, played for Queen's Park at the turn of the century and had the nickname 'Toffee Bob'. Anderson's name was a corruption of this as he was also in the confectionery business.

4 Emilio Pacione was a regular goalscorer for United. He scored 33 goals between 1945 and 1950. Frank Quinn scored 90 times between 1948 and 1954. Peter MacKay scored 238 in 202 games over roughly the same period.

5 Dundee also had a notable first round victory over Celtic, 2–1 at Dens, in season 1946–47.

6 Bobby Flavell, who had come from Hearts, had also played in South America with Bogotá, where one of his team-mates was Alfredo di Stefano.

7 Albert Henderson, who had a long playing career with Dundee and St Mirren and went on to manage Arbroath.

TWELVE

If the 1920s and '30s were times of political revolution, the 1950s and '60s will be remembered for their social revolution, the 'Revolt into Style', as George Melly has described the period. In 1953, however, international relations stood deadlocked in the 'Cold War' and neither America's new President, Eisenhower, nor Stalin's successors, Malenkov and Bulganin, looked as though they were going to do very much to alter that state of affairs.

Dundee East had a new Labour MP in George Thomson; Cowie and Steel played for Scotland at Wembley in a 2–2 draw; and Bobby Ancell became manager of Dunfermline, with Andy Dickson as trainer. Billy Steel, unfortunately, was beginning to lose the place at Dens and his departure to the United States would not be long delayed. Elsewhere two ex-Dundee juniors, Jackie Mudie and Ewen Fenton, played their part in Blackpool's 'Matthews Cup Final' victory; Mount Everest was climbed for the first time; and the country celebrated the coronation of Elizabeth II.

United went out of the Scottish Cup in the first round to Berwick Rangers, losing 3–2 at Tannadice, Dens Park had its biggest ever crowd[1] and in May 1953 Dundee toured South Africa where they were greeted by some 5,000 people at the airport. This tour helped establish a link between the city's footballing fraternity and that country. Two right-backs in particular would benefit from the long trek. A third, Gerry Follon, was involved in an interesting local dispute. Follon was a schoolteacher in Dundee and after some debate was barred from the South African tour by the local authority – not on moral grounds, as might have been the case during the apartheid era, but because teachers were in short supply.

In 1954 United suffered a record 12–1 defeat at the hands of Motherwell and Dundee FC faced a similar humiliation soon afterwards when they lost 3–0 to 'C' division Berwick Rangers in the third round of the Cup. Duncan Hutchison was re-elected to the United board (he had first been co-opted as a director the previous year); Scot Symon became manager of Rangers in succession to Bill Struth; and another ex-Ranger, Willie Thornton, was invited to take over as manager at Dens (Anderson had resigned through ill health). At Tannadice, Peter MacKay's goalscoring feats had attracted the attention of the local Burnley scout, Jimmy Scott, and he was transferred to that club. But United had a ready-made replacement in the burly, young Dundonian Johnny Coyle, and when Reg Smith was appointed manager in succession to McFadyen, United's prospects looked somewhat brighter. Smith, I imagine, would have been rather disappointed at being overlooked for the Dundee job and so not for the first (or the last) time, a 'Dundee' man took the short walk down Tannadice Street.

Scottish football in the early 1950s was a mixture of full-time and part-time players, but players, managers and coaches were beginning to adopt a more professional attitude and the necessity of such an approach was underlined when Hungary – the 'Magical Magyars', including the brilliant forwards Sandor, Kocsis, Hidegkuti, Puskas and Fenyvesi – visited Hampden. The advice of *Sporting Post* columnist 'Rambler' to the Scotland team was to 'come out fighting' but, like everyone else who played the game more or less fairly, Scotland were taken apart by the Hungarians. The following week 'Rambler', obviously in a state of shock, gibbered: 'I think we have a good way to go before we reach the end of the road towards the top again'!

Two significant additions were made to the United board in 1955 in Johnstone Grant, a haulage contractor, and George Fox, a chartered accountant; but both United and Dundee were languishing in mid-table positions and United were later said to be £10,000 in debt at this time. Both clubs continued to enjoy good individual performances from the likes of Coyle, who was now one of the most consistent goalscorers in the 'B' Division, and Cowie, one of the most polished midfield players in Division 'A' and who attracted a bid from Cardiff City. Cowie was reluctant to move for domestic reasons, however, and Cardiff switched their attentions to his clubmate, centre-half Danny Malloy, who duly signed for £17,500.

Hibs at their first attempt reached the semi-final of the new European Cup (1956)[2] and in the League Cup that year Dundee FC and United, drawn against each other in the quarter-finals, played home and away. Dundee players were: Brown; Reid and Irvine; Henderson, McKenzie and Cowie; Chalmers, Black, Merchant, O'Hara and Christie. United were represented by: Edmiston; Young and Briggs; Will, Cross and Stewart; Sturrock, Aikman, John Coyle, Reid and Maurice Milne.

Dundee FC, as the full-timers, were seen to be much fitter in the first leg. This they won by seven goals to three, with Jim Chalmers scoring four. But in the second leg United, strengthened by new right-back signing Davie Gray, showed that they were always a difficult team to beat at Tannadice and won 2–1. An anonymous fan was quoted in the *Record* as saying that had United gone into the first game with more concentration, they would have reached the semis – thereby underlining the conventional United wisdom that they were always as good a side as Dundee. In the semi-final, the game against Partick Thistle was drawn 0–0, with 17-year-old Alan Cousin coming into contention for a place for the first time, but the replay, under the Ibrox lights, was lost 3–2.

Hugh Robertson, a left-winger from Auchinleck Talbot, was the next young hopeful to sign for Dundee, and Bobby Cox the next to make the first team. Rock 'n' roll had arrived (although it would be another two years before Tommy Steele was quite badly injured by ecstatic fans following a concert in the Caird Hall), but while it was evidently great to be young, the local headlines belonged to neither pop stars nor footballers. Instead they concentrated on a 21-year-old Dundee boxer named Dick McTaggart.

McTaggart, an apprentice butcher and one of six boxing brothers, had slowly been picking up a reputation as an amateur lightweight. As ABA champion he was one of five unanimous choices for the British Olympics team (Melbourne, December 1956) and not only did he win the gold medal at his weight, he also received the prestigious Val Barker Trophy as the most stylish boxer at the games. Two thousand Dundonians made his return triumphal and he also showed the trophy at Dundee FC's next home game.

Johnny Coyle carried on in season 1956–57 where he had left off the previous year and once again he was the Second Division's second top scorer. But any possible moves were suspended when Reg Smith was suddenly offered the Falkirk job in succession to Bob Shankly, who had left Brockville after 23 years as player and manager. This was a disappointment for the United fans, as the former English cap had embarked upon a long-term plan for the club. To a certain extent the feeling was mutual, for before he left, Smith paid tribute to the United board for trying to hold on to their players. Falkirk, however, were a 'bigger' club than United at the time and so the move represented an opportunity to try out some of his more progressive ideas – ideas which bore fruit almost immediately, for in his very first Scottish Cup campaign as manager (1957) he actually brought the Cup to Brockville, beating Kilmarnock 2–1 in extra time of the final replay! The Falkirk team included the brother of a Dundee FC player (Eddie O'Hara); the two men who had just left Dundee FC (George Merchant and Andy Irvine); a man who would subsequently play for Dundee FC (Bert Slater); and one who would do likewise for United (Doug Moran, scorer of the winning goal). Add Bob Shankly and Reg Smith to that list and it makes most interesting reading. Shankly now moved to Third Lanark.

No managerial appointment was made immediately at Tannadice, thus leaving Ally Gallacher (assistant manager) and Archie Coats (trainer, ex-Dundee) in charge of the team. However later that year (1957) the job was filled by Tommy Gray, the former Dundee player and Arbroath manager, and one of his early duties was to transfer Coyle to Clyde, for £8,000. Johnny had scored 45 goals, 41 goals and 20 goals to date in three seasons and he, too, proved to be the missing link at his new club which, remarkably, won the 1958 Scottish Cup with Coyle scoring the winning goal in the final against Hibs. Sometime, one could not help but think, some of his outgoing luck was bound to make the return journey.

Hearts, with Dave Mackay as captain, won the First Division championship; Elvis Presley was drafted; and the Busby Babes – the brilliant young Manchester United team – were decimated by an air crash at Munich.[3] Busby himself had just accepted the job as Scotland team manager and his club side, which had reached the semi-final of the European Cup, would possibly have been the first British team to win that trophy. Football went into a state of shock. It came back to life, however, in the summer of 1958 when the phenomenal 17-year-old Brazilian, Pelé, appeared in the

World Cup finals in Sweden and performed at the very highest level.

Dundee United also discovered a fine young player that season (1957–58) in Ronnie Yeats, a centre-half and giant of an Aberdonian around whom a new team would be built, though it would take another two years and two changes of management. Similar changes were afoot at Dunfermline FC, whom Bobby Ancell left for Motherwell to be succeeded by Andy Dickson; and in Los Angeles a young starlet named Joan Collins was quoted as saying that she never allowed her 'dates' to say their 'goodnights' in her Hollywood flat, but took her leave of them on the doorstep. Oh, really?

Season 1958–59 began promisingly for both clubs and when Dundee FC won 2–0 at Ibrox the *Daily Record* said, 'Dundee have the makings of a team that could win the Scottish Cup . . .' By now Alan Cousin was a Scottish League cap; a fine young player from Westrigg Bluebell, Alex Hamilton, had taken over 'Shug' Reid's right-back position; and an outstanding prospect named Jimmy Gabriel was at centre-half. Dundee FC then picked up a top-class young Fifer, 15-year-old Andy Penman, a Scottish Schoolboy cap who had been unhappy with his first choice, Everton. All in all, things actually did seem to be quite healthy at Dens – when disaster struck.

In the first round of the Scottish Cup (31 January 1959) Dundee FC were drawn away to Fraserburgh, a Highland League club consisting of the usual mix of tradesmen, students and others. Dundee lined up: Brown; Hamilton and Cox; Henderson, Gabriel and Cowie; Curlett, Bonthrone, Cousin, Sneddon and Robertson. The *Record* confidently backed its earlier judgement, predicting that Dundee would 'saunter to success'. In fact, they sauntered to failure, for in a nightmare match they lost a goal in 46 minutes which proved to be decisive.

Emergency bells were now ringing at Dens Park and it was expected they would be forced into the transfer market. Davie Sneddon, signed from Kilwinning Rangers in 1954, went to Preston for £12,000 in April 1959 and two months later Bill Brown, arguably Scotland's finest ever goalkeeper, followed Dave Mackay to Tottenham Hotspur for £17,500.

United were not involved in much finance, but they too were in trouble in that they had slumped to third bottom place in the Second Division.

NOTES

1 A crowd of 43,024 watched Dundee v Rangers in February 1953.

2 Aberdeen actually won the 1954–55 League, but entry to the first Champions' Cup was by invitation.

3 Manchester United were beaten 5–1 at Dens in a friendly in 1956. Their team contained a number of star players and a young Bobby Charlton, whose début it was for the club.

THIRTEEN

The year 1959 marks the beginning of what might be called the 'modern era' in Dundee football and, just as managerial changes precipitated new eras in the 1920s and '40s, so it was in the 1960s.

Although manager Willie Thornton left Dundee FC for Partick Thistle in September 1959, he did so for domestic reasons and acknowledged that he was leaving a club healthier both in footballing and financial terms than the one he was joining. With the transfer of Bill Brown, Dundee FC were in a sound financial position and they used the money to install floodlights and build the covered enclosure opposite the main stand. United were at something of a low ebb in their football, but they too were reasonably healthy financially now, thanks mainly to the success of their Taypools operation which had begun in 1956 and which would also provide the money to pay for ground improvements. The ex-Dundee full-back and trainer, Andy McCall, had taken over from Tommy Gray as manager at Tannadice, but was singularly unsuccessful and on 6 July 1959 United made a new managerial appointment which was to have far-reaching consequences.

Jerry Kerr had captained the club during their successful wartime Cup run and when his playing career was over he managed first Berwick Rangers and then Alloa, where he signed two brilliant inside-forwards who proceeded to hand out regular footballing lessons to other Second Division clubs – United included. One was the legendary John White, who would soon leave Falkirk for Spurs before, tragically, being killed by lightning, and the other Denis Gillespie, who was one of Kerr's earliest signings and one of the most significant. On 16 April 1958 Alloa, managed by Kerr, had beaten United 7–1 at Tannadice, with White scoring five and Gillespie two. Jerry Kerr's one promise to the United board on taking up the appointment was that he would improve their (third bottom) league position.

At Dens the manager's job went to the now successful Third Lanark boss, Bob Shankly who, it was reported, had earlier turned down the United job. He inherited a number of fine players including Pat Liney, Alex Hamilton, Bobby Cox, Ian Ure, Andy Penman, Alan Cousin, Alan Gilzean and Hugh Robertson – although some of them still had to establish themselves in the first team.

Season 1959–60, however, belonged to United. Happy with his goalkeeper Alec Brown, centre-half Ronnie Yeats and right-winger Bobby Norris, Kerr at once set about strengthening his team in other positions. Apart from Gillespie, right-half Peter Smith came from Hearts, inside-right Jim Irvine and right-half Tommy Graham from junior football, left-half Stewart Fraser from the Army. And if Yeats was unavailable because of his Army duties, he had a capable deputy in another young Aberdonian, Doug Smith, although Kerr did sign a third centre-half, David Kidd, from Alloa. Right-half Tommy Neilson was then signed from East Fife and he was joined by another wing-half or inside-forward, Dave Whytock[1] from Brechin City. With Eric Walker then coming from Alloa and Gibby Ormond (brother of Willie) from Airdrie, Kerr's side was almost complete and at the turn of the year United, in second place, and their league leaders St Johnstone, drew 1–1 at Perth before

16,000 spectators. This was obviously going to be the club's strongest promotion challenge since 1930–31.

Yeats, in particular, was proving to be a tower of strength, and with the arrival of RAF man Jimmy Briggs at left-back, the defence became more or less settled. Recognising the need for a final push, however, Kerr than pulled out an ace in Albion Rovers' top-scoring centre-forward Tommy Campbell. His specialist touch enabled the Terrors to sustain their challenge.

Things were also looking up in the local newspaper, for Tommy Gallacher, the ex-Dundee half-back, now became football correspondent for the *Courier*, and coverage improved dramatically in its style and content. In spite of continuing complaints of a Dundee FC bias in the paper, it was Gallacher who first promoted United to a regular 'top spot' in the sports page if he thought their game merited it. In one match, for example, United had an important 3–1 victory over Montrose at Links Park and his 'counter attraction', said the *Courier*, kept the attendance at Dens Park down to 7,000. United were on their way.

On the same day, Jerry Kerr departed from a personal rule by signing an outside-right named Walter Carlyle from Shettleston Juniors without having seen him play. He was in for a surprise! Besides being a good player, the fair-haired Carlyle turned out to be a tremendous character and crowd-pleaser who became famous for goals from 'impossible' angles and other eccentric play.

Dundee FC, meanwhile, transferred 19-year-old Jimmy Gabriel to Everton for an incredible £30,000 and his replacement was another striking, blond-haired half-back from Ayr, Ian Ure; Everton's neighbours Liverpool, now managed by Shankly's brother Bill, handselled the Dundee FC floodlights (Dundee won 1–0); and Yeats, Campbell and Ormond got a game for the Second Division Select against the Under-23s. Such was Yeats' importance to United, he would occasionally be flown from Aldershot, or even Germany; but Kerr's judgement was sound for, with Queen of the South and Hamilton stumbling in the run-up, United reached the last game needing to beat Berwick Rangers at Tannadice to join champions St Johnstone in the First Division. They lined up: Brown; Graham and McFadyen (Briggs was injured); Neilson, Yeats and Fraser; Norris, Irvine, Campbell, Gillespie and Ormond. Sixteen thousand people attended the match and the team was on £500 'talent money' to be shared among them if they won – which they duly did, by one goal to nil, Tommy Campbell scoring in the ninth minute.[2]

NOTES

1 Whytock failed to gain a regular place in the first team but had a successful academic career and was the prospective Labour candidate for Dundee East when he was killed in a car crash prior to the 1979 General Election.

2 Andy Dickson became physiotherapist at Tannadice and Sammy Kean trainer at Dens Park.

FOURTEEN

The summer of 1960 saw Dick McTaggart collect another Olympic medal, this time a bronze in Rome; Scotland hosted one of the best football games of all time when Real Madrid defeated Eintracht 7–3 in the European Cup final at Hampden; and United's man-of-the-moment Jerry Kerr kept up his astonishing work rate by visiting the Frankfurt club after the final to try to learn something of their methods. He also signed an Italian-born goalkeeper, Roland Ugolini, from Wrexham and promoted him, along with Walter Carlyle, to the first team; and the club won their first match 2–1 away to Stirling Albion.

At Dens Park, Bob Shankly signed a cultured right-half, Bobby Seith, from English champions Burnley; chose Pat Liney as the successor to Bill Brown (one of Liney's rivals had been the curiously named Charlie Pllu); and watched Alan Gilzean embark upon his goalscoring odyssey for the club. Dundee FC looked on paper to be the stronger of the city teams, but it was United who won the first derby match 3–1 at Tannadice, and they then briefly topped the First Division on goal average. Reg Smith, now the manager of Millwall, was said to be interested in a young Hamilton Accies right-winger, Jim McLean (he eventually went to Clyde); Ian McColl, astonishingly, was asked to become

Scotland team manager whilst still a Rangers player. Meanwhile John Fitzgerald Kennedy became the first Roman Catholic President of the United States. He wouldn't have got a game for Rangers, though, as the Ibrox club continued to pursue an anti-Catholic policy.

Neilly Mochan signed for United from Celtic, although he was approaching the veteran stage; Bobby Wishart was brought to Dens Park from Aberdeen; and Dundee FC played Valenciennes in the new Friendship Cup. Jimmy Hill, the ex-Fulham player, was making waves as chairman of the English Players' Union and a new deal was on the way for footballers in both England and Scotland. Tannadice began its long-awaited facelift with an L-shaped stand and floodlights; and Dundee itself saw some dramatic changes as the old heart was torn out of the city to make way for the new Overgate development.

At Dens an era ended when Bob Shankly announced the departure of that great servant, Doug Cowie – the last of George Anderson's signings – and in doing so, Shankly gave notice that he had definite plans for what *his* team would be and how it would play. The short-ball game at which Cowie excelled would give way to a new style geared towards the strong front-runners Cousin and Gilzean. Cowie had given 446 performances in 15 years and had earned himself 23 caps. He now moved to Morton as player-coach.[1]

Yuri Gagarin of Russia was the first man in space; Frank Haffey of Celtic was almost the first goalkeeper in space when he lost nine playing for Scotland at Wembley; and the astutely managed Tottenham Hotspur won the English Cup and League 'double', the first team to do so since Aston Villa in 1897.

United also finished one point ahead of Dundee FC at the end of their first season in the First Division for 40 years, but it was the Dark Blues who had the more settled team and when Gordon Smith, the 'Stanley Matthews' of Scottish football, signed for them on a free transfer from Hearts in June 1961, Shankly's jigsaw was complete. Neither Dundee FC nor United qualified from their League Cup section, however, and United's balance sheet showed a loss of £13,754, so a transfer was on the cards and the obvious candidate was the brilliant Yeats. He eventually moved to Liverpool and is generally recognised as the first rock upon which Bill Shankly built that great modern club. The fee was £30,000. Ure, Gilzean, Penman and Gillespie got Scottish League caps – in Gillespie's case it was a first for United and he was also named in Scotland's World Cup pool along with Hamilton, Seith, Ure, Gilzean and Robertson. Indeed, of the Dundee FC side, only Pat Liney remained uncapped and this was reflected in the club's league position as they raced to the top of the table, at one stage going 19 games without defeat.

Inevitably, Rangers were not far away and with games in hand, so the match at Ibrox on 11 November 1961 was eagerly anticipated. On that foggy afternoon, Dundee FC demonstrated their championship potential by recording one of the greatest victories in their history. Alan Gilzean scored four, and Andy Penman one, in a 5–1 away triumph. Membership of their supporters' club soared. However, any manager will tell you that one good league result wins nothing and so it was the results of other matches which indicated Dundee's consistency to the fans and the fact that they really did have a good chance that year. Early in the season, for example, the club played magnificently at Fir Park, Motherwell, to beat Bobby Ancell's ever-skilful side 4–2, and the week after the Ibrox result they fought tooth and nail to beat Raith Rovers 5–4 at Dens in a fantastic finish. Further, a first-round Scottish Cup defeat at the hands of St Mirren, whilst temporarily shaking their confidence, served to focus their attention on the league challenge.

At Tannadice, Stewart Fraser was turning in some great

performances with Yeats' successor Doug Smith, and was recognised by a Scottish League cap, but all eyes were fixed on the Dundee players and, ironically, United did them a good turn in March 1962 when they registered their first-ever victory (1–0) at Ibrox. Dundee FC then consolidated their position with a 2–1 away win at Tannadice on the holiday Monday, but the crucial matches took place on Wednesday, 25 April. That night Aberdeen beat Rangers 1–0 at Pittodrie; and when Liney saved a penalty at Dens in a 2–0 victory over St Mirren, it became known as 'the night that turned the championship'. Only 15 players were used by Dundee FC in the entire season, the famous team: Liney; Hamilton and Cox (captain); Seith, Ure and Wishart; Smith, Penman, Cousin, Gilzean and Robertson; plus Craig Brown (six games), Bobby Waddell (four), Alec Stuart (two) and George McCreadie (two). Five of them originally came from the general Tayside area.

Dundee FC met St Johnstone at Muirton in the final game of the season, knowing that victory would give them the flag, and they won it in style by three goals to nil (Gilzean 2, Penman). St Johnstone, unfortunately, were relegated as a result, but this could not dampen the enthusiasm of the Dundee fans and, coincidentally, Liverpool won the English Second Division championship. It was brother Bob's team which was bound for Europe that year, however.

* * *

Dundee FC had travelled only occasionally abroad since the early 1920s, when William McIntosh took them to Spain.[2] George Anderson saw the value of such travel and took the club to Belgium in the late '40s and to Turkey and the Middle East in the early '50s. But recent travel had been fairly restricted and Shankly made good use of an opportunity to test his side against European opposition by accepting an offer to play in a close-season tournament in New York (1962). Dundee's results were disappointing, but the defence at least benefited from the experiment of playing to different systems. Shankly was not particularly happy with Pat Liney's form, however, and decided to buy another keeper, Bert Slater, who himself had lost his first-team place with Liverpool.

In the second round of the European Cup (1962–63) Dundee FC drew FC Cologne, German champions and one of the sides fancied to win the competition. Dundee's League Cup performances had been disappointing and no one could have foreseen what was to happen in the first match, played at Dens on 5 September. Dundee lined up with their recognised side – but with Slater in goal – and they proceeded to run up a 3–0 advantage before the German goalkeeper was injured in an innocuous clash with Cousin. At half-time, with the score 5–0, he was taken off suffering from concussion and Dundee eventually won by eight goals to one. This, of course, was an exhilarating result for Dundee fans and Scottish football, for the match had not been a roughhouse; but the rumblings from the German camp suggested they thought otherwise, and that the return might see a very different result 'if, say, the Dundee goalkeeper was injured' – a quote actually attributed to the Cologne coach by the German newspapers.

It was unlikely that the man had the gift of second sight, but it was an ominous sign, and when the stretcher-bearers took up their position behind the Dundee FC goal in the return match at the Müngersdorf Stadium, the travelling support feared the worst. In an early attack Slater was deliberately kicked on the head and had to be replaced by Penman, although the goalkeeper refused to be taken to hospital and later resumed on the wing. Penman played well, but had to face a penalty with the score at 4–0. Had that been converted, Cologne would probably have gone on to win. It was missed, however, and with Slater back in goal, Dundee finished the match 8–5 ahead on aggregate. But worse was to follow.

When it became obvious that their team could not overhaul the Dark Blues, hundreds of German fans encircled the pitch. In the absence of any police action, they laid into the Dundee players, sometimes with chairs, as they tried to reach the dressing-rooms some 50 yards away, at the end of the match.[3] It was despicable treatment and the Dundee FC board refused to attend the post-match reception.

In the second round their opponents were Sporting Club of Lisbon and from the first match, played away, they returned with a creditable 1–0 defeat. At Dens the crowd was 31,000 and with Ian Ure in great form at the back, the Dundee forwards had a field day, scoring four times with one reply. United, meantime, inaugurated their floodlights with a match against Rangers (9 November 1962) and Carlyle scored one of his 'specials'. But everything was riding on Dundee FC and Europe and in the next round they gave what was arguably their best-ever performance abroad.

On 6 March 1963, they visited the Belgian champions Anderlecht and confounded the soccer world with a 4–1 away victory, including two goals from Gilzean. The home match was therefore something of a formality, but this was also won, by two goals to one and before a capacity 40,000 crowd.

The semi-finalists in the European Cup of 1963 were Benfica, also of Lisbon, AC Milan, Feyenoord of Rotterdam and Dundee FC – an achievement which speaks for itself – and the Dark Blues drew Milan, with the first game to be played in the more fashionable Italian city. AC had players such as Rivera, Maldini and Trappatoni, and had knocked out English champions Ipswich in the second round.

However the final was to be played at Wembley that year and Dundee knew that if they could surmount the semi-final hurdle, they would have a good chance of actually winning the Cup.

It was not to be, however. Captain Bobby Cox was injured and his place went to the young Alec Stuart and, given that an all-out defensive effort might be required in the first game, Hugh Robertson was replaced on the left-wing by the more versatile Doug Houston. In the first half, in spite of refereeing which denied the Dundee players any physical contact whatsoever, the team performed well and a Cousin header equalised an earlier goal from Sani. In the second half, however, a combination of a barrage of flash bulbs blinding Dundee's attack whenever they were in front of goal, and a cross-ball game punishing their defence, led to the loss of four more goals.

It is always easy to blame biased refereeing or underhand tactics in such matches, but an incident some five days later illustrates the volatility of the Italian game at the time and the atmosphere in which it was often played. During a game between Naples and Modena the crowd rioted and smashed the posts. One person was killed and 89 injured. Fortunately, things were not so bad at Dens Park in the return match with Milan, which Dundee won 1–0, but Gilzean was sent off in the face of provocation and even Gordon Smith[4] was seen to retaliate once – a very rare sight indeed.

AC Milan went on to win the European Cup and Spurs the Cup-Winners' Cup. United finished seventh in the Scottish League, two places above Dundee FC. And the 'Swinging Sixties' made their first tentative moves with the Beatles and Christine Keeler rocking British youth and the Conservative government respectively.

NOTES

1 Cowie received no benefit game and his experience was later cited by Ian
  Ure as one of the reasons why he had to seek a transfer and more money.
2 Spanish results, 1923: 2–0 v Real Madrid; 3–0 and 1–0 v Valencia; 3–0 and
  1–1 v Bilbao; 0–2 and 1–3 v Barcelona.
3 Some British servicemen stationed in Germany were at the match and came
  to the assistance of the Dundee players.
4 Smith had now played in the European Cup for a record three different
  clubs: Hibs, Hearts and Dundee.

FIFTEEN

It had been known since the late '50s that the future of British football teams in terms of both earning power and prestige lay in the European competitions, and these games also served to give players some idea of their individual standing in the international game. The Dundee FC players who made the greatest impression in Europe in the early '60s were Ian Ure and Alan Gilzean.

Ure had originally come from Ayr, where he attended the rugby-playing Ayr Academy and so he was a late developer in football, but his strong physique and aerial power marked him out as a defender of international class. The abolition of the maximum wage in England made it certain that his future lay south of the border. This was a time when a number of top-class Scottish players made that move and Ure's choice, following a brief dispute with Dundee FC (during which he attempted to claim unemployment benefit)[1] was Arsenal, then managed by Billy Wright. The fee was £62,500 and his replacement in the Dundee team was his understudy, George Ryden.

Gilzean, a Coupar Angus man like his nineteenth-century namesakes, whose goalscoring feats[2] and heading skills in particular will always live with anyone fortunate enough to have seen them, played for Dundee FC for one more season. But it was inevitable that he too would move, and he was transferred in December 1964 to Tottenham Hotspur for £72,500. His replacement was another outstanding footballer, only this time a ball-playing inside-forward who seemed to have the ability to beat men in slow motion – Charlie Cooke, who came from Aberdeen FC for £30,000.

United, however, were not standing still at this time. Alternating between an all-black and red and white 'Arsenal' strip, they continued to consolidate their First Division status and, most importantly, to stay in profit. Duncan Hutchison became chairman, succeeding Ernest Robertson. In the wider world, Peter Doig was elected Labour MP for Dundee West (Britain would have a Labour government under Harold Wilson the following year) and, on 22 November 1963, President Kennedy was assassinated in Dallas, Texas.

Dundee FC reached the final of the Scottish Cup that season (1963–64) but lost by two late goals to Rangers in a 3–1 defeat. The team was Slater; Hamilton and Cox; Seith, Ryden and Stuart; Penman, Cousin, Cameron, Gilzean and Robertson. But as Rangers also won the league that year, the Dark Blues qualified for the 1964–65 European Cup-Winners' Cup.

Dundee's goalscorer in the final was new centre-forward Kenny 'On-the-Spot' Cameron, who would later end up at Tannadice, first as a player and then as coach, and United also introduced some new faces around this time in goalkeeping rivals Donald MacKay and Sandy Davie, utility player Benny Rooney and teenage forwards Ian Mitchell and Frank Munro. The Terrors also began to establish something of a hoodoo over their local rivals in derby. More of that later, for the main topic of interest at Tannadice, as at Dens, in the mid-1960s was the continent of Europe – only it was not in competition that United made their initial impact, but in the transfer market.

Following the example set by Hall Stewart[3] at Morton,

the enterprising Jerry Kerr discovered that there was a pool of talent available in Scandinavia and, on account of local regulations governing professional football, at comparatively little cost. Kerr's first signing, and arguably his best, was a classy Swedish left-winger, Orjan Persson, who initially signed amateur forms. He was followed by fellow-countryman Lennart Wing, Danes Finn Dossing and Mogens Berg, and Norwegian Finn Seemann. The Scandinavians were both popular and successful as players. On 11 September 1965 Dossing scored a hat-trick in a 5–0 United victory over Dundee at Dens and Persson eventually moved to Rangers, with whom he also enjoyed success.

In the European Cup-Winners' Cup, Dundee FC drew 2–2 with Zaragossa at Dens but lost 4–3 on aggregate and Shankly saw this result as demonstrating that he had achieved all he could for Dundee Football Club. He now moved on to manage Hibs, replacing Jock Stein who had gone to Celtic. But Shankly left his successor Bobby Ancell some fine young players, including Ally Donaldson, Steve Murray, Alec Totten, George Stewart and Jocky Scott.

Bobby Seith was now appointed coach at Dens; Celtic's first non-Catholic manager won the Scottish Cup for them at his first attempt; another provincial side, Kilmarnock, won the League (1964–65); United beat Dundee FC twice in the Summer Cup and reached the final only to lose to Motherwell on aggregate;[4] Hugh Robertson went to Dunfermline Athletic and became the first Scot to play in all three European tournaments; and Scotland failed to qualify for the 1966 World Cup finals.

In December 1965, Dundee FC signed Jim McLean, the Clyde inside-forward. Originally from Larkhall, McLean was one of three footballing brothers who enjoyed varying success as players but who, like the Shankly brothers before them, would become better known as managers. At the turn of the year, United were in fourth place in the First Division, their best mid-term showing to date, and they finished the season in fifth position, thus qualifying for a place in the Inter-Cities Fairs Cup. Dundee FC finished ninth and when Charlie Cooke announced that he wished to break his contract with the club (he eventually went to Chelsea for £72,000), the well-known Scots football journalist Hugh Taylor was moved to voice his disgust at the player's decision in the *Daily Record*.

In an astonishing article, Taylor first said that he had been a Dundee fan but would now switch his allegiance to Tannadice. And he followed this up with the pronouncement that he was fed up with those who carped at the success of Rangers and Celtic. The Old Firm, he opined, were 'entitled to rule Scottish soccer' because they 'kept it alive'. He did get one thing right when he forecast that Dundee FC, by transferring their star players, would now suffer at the turnstiles and, to my knowledge, he was the first to coin the term 'the New Firm' – referring to Tommy Docherty's young Scotland team of 1971. But that's about all.

Dundee FC could not possibly have held on to their star players and to some extent were victims of their own success. How they invested the (net) £250,000 received for Brown, Gabriel, Ure, Gilzean and Cooke, however, might have stood closer scrutiny.

In any event, it was now United's turn to savour European glory for the first time. They had got their chance in the Fairs Cup as a result of an extension of the Scottish representation to three clubs, and Kerr took them to Scandinavia for a close-season preparation. Even the most optimistic fan, however, could not have anticipated the pay-off, for in the very first round they drew the holders, Barcelona, with the first game to be played in Spain.

England had won the World Cup that year with a 4–3–3 formation and it was this which Kerr deployed with brilliant success. On 26 October 1966, in their first-ever competitive

European match, they beat Barcelona 2–1 (away) with goals from Billy Hainey and Finn Seemann (penalty). In the return game Ian Mitchell opened for United and the ex-Thistle striker Hainey made it two from a speculative effort. The away result was hailed as 'the best ever . . . achieved by a Scottish side abroad' and the aggregate victory, said the *Record*, would 'ring around Europe'. It would not be for the last time.[5]

United were in a particularly healthy condition at this time with Taypools worth £30,000 a year to them, and gates were rising at Tannadice whilst they fell elsewhere. In the second round they drew another big name in Juventus of Turin and in the first (away) leg Seemann almost scored in the first minute. Disaster struck in the second half, however, and the game was lost 3–0. At Tannadice the score was 1–0 for United.

This was the season (1966–67) in which Celtic would win the European Cup but there was almost equal drama on the domestic front. Bob Seith became trainer-coach of Rangers in December 1966, but almost before he had time to take off his Dundee FC blazer, Rangers had suffered one of the worst results in their history – going down 1–0 (away) to Jock Wallace's team, Berwick Rangers, in the first round of the Scottish Cup. Heads were bound to roll and besides players George McLean and Jim Forrest (McLean came to Dundee in part exchange for Andy Penman), manager Scot Symon also got 'the boot' later that year, in spite of the fact that he had taken them to the final of the Cup-Winners' Cup (1967). Seith then resigned in protest, saying that he 'no longer wished to be part of an organisation which can treat a loyal servant so badly'.

Dundee United beat Celtic home and away in the Celts' glory season, the only club to do so; Alex Ferguson became the star of his club, Dunfermline; and Davie White, when appointed the new manager of Rangers, signed that striker for the Light Blues. Orjan Persson was then also transferred to Rangers, with Davy Wilson and Wilson Wood coming to Tannadice.

By a quirky ruling, Dundee FC, who finished sixth in the league (United were eighth), were given a place in the 1967–68 Fairs Cup – only one representative could come from each city and this debarred Clyde – and in the first round they defeated DWS Amsterdam 4–2 on aggregate, with Jim McLean scoring two in the home tie.[6]

Dundee FC reached the final of the League Cup in 1967, but lost two goals to Celtic in the first 11 minutes and, in spite of a good performance by George McLean, went down 5–3 (G. McLean 2, J. McLean). They lined up: Arrol; R. Wilson and Houston; Murray, Stewart and Stuart; Campbell, J. McLean and S. Wilson;[7] G. McLean and Bryce.

In the second round of the Fairs Cup, Dundee FC beat Royal Liege 3–1 at Dens and scored a remarkable 4–1 victory with George McLean getting all four. McLean, like Walter Carlyle, was a saint one day and a sinner the next, but was another who always gave at least entertainment value for money. Bobby Seith now went to manage Preston; Bob Shankly's Hibs side included Peter Cormack, Pat Stanton and Colin Stein, and the popular press reported that Scotland was living in an 'age of violence'. There had apparently been 49 murders in ten months in the country and the main focus of the sensational reporting was one James 'Baby Face' Boyle, aged 24, from the Gorbals. In fact, there was a great deal of social upheaval and violence throughout the world at this time with the Vietnam war at its height, the assassinations of Martin Luther King and Bobby Kennedy in America and the Russian invasion of Czechoslovakia.

In the quarter-finals of the European Fairs Cup, Dundee FC defeated FC Zurich 1–0 in both matches and Don

Revie's fine Leeds United team put out Hibs, so the scene was set for an all-British semi-final. Reaching that stage was a really fine achievement for Dundee – 'Europe's Ghost Team', as the description went – but the times had changed as far as the fans were concerned. Only 41,000 in total watched the first three home ties and the old enthusiasm could not be summoned. Away goals also now counted double in this tournament and a Paul Madeley counter, although equalised by Bobby Wilson, virtually saw Leeds through. The Yorkshire club won the return tie 1–0 and went on to win the competition.

Frank Munro went to Aberdeen; Doug Smith missed his first game in four and a half years; and Denis Gillespie was described as the best (fully) uncapped player in Scotland. Bobby Ancell 'blooded' two young strikers, John Duncan and Roddy Georgeson and, feeling that a younger man should also be in the manager's chair, stepped down himself in favour of John Prentice in October 1969. Jim McLean was then transferred to Kilmarnock and men walked on the moon, although the two events were unconnected.

NOTES

1 Three Dundee FC players, Marsh, McNab and Gilmour, had also sought recourse to Social Security in 1932, before the dispute was settled.

2 Gilzean broke Alec Stott's club goalscoring record by scoring 53 goals in season 1963–64.

3 Stewart was a Dundonian who had assisted George Anderson in a personal capacity.

4 Motherwell 3, United 1; United 1, Motherwell 0.

5 United's team in Barcelona was: Davie; Miller and Briggs; Neilson, Smith and wing; Seemann, Hainey, Mitchell, Gillespie and Persson.

6 In domestic competition Dundee FC were said by the *Daily Record* to be 'dreadfully disappointing' in a match against United and 'unlikely to

challenge Celtic'. It is revealing that the prospect of United challenging Celtic was not even considered by the Glasgow press, as recently as this.

7 Billy Campbell and Sammy Wilson were both capped by Northern Ireland and Bobby Wilson by the Scottish League. Alec Bryce came from Clyde and John Arrol from Stirling Albion.

SIXTEEN

John Prentice had had an eventful career in football. As a player he captained the Scottish Cup-winning Falkirk side in 1957 and as a manager he was briefly in charge of the Scotland team before being sacked for investigating the possibility of another job in Canada. His first season at Dens, however, will probably only be remembered for the transfer of Jim McLean to Kilmarnock where he teamed up with younger brother Tommy. Dundee finished tenth that year and United a most creditable fifth, with Kenny Cameron the first United player to top the scoring charts since Johnny Coyle.

The following season United drew Newcastle United in the first round of the Fairs Cup and, in spite of two great performances by Alec Reid, went down 2–1 at home and 1–0 away. But the Tangerines[1] maintained their league position and Dundee FC were not far behind. The Dark Blues also reached the semi-final of the Scottish Cup, but went out 2–1 to a great Celtic team who then beat Leeds United on the way to their second European Cup final (which they lost 2–1 to Feyenoord).

With Richard Nixon as President the Americans now extended the Vietnam war in Cambodia; Paul McCartney announced the break-up of the Beatles; and Aberdeen won

the Scottish Cup with Dundonian Davie Robb and ex-
Dundee FC player Derek McKay playing prominent parts.
Edward Heath's Tories formed a government; United's
talented wing-half or inside-forward Jim Henry was capped
by the Scottish League against the League of Ireland; and
Jim McLean returned to Dens as first-team coach (April
1970) on the understanding that he would not appear for
them as a player.

In the 1970–71 Fairs Cup, United drew Grasshoppers of
Zurich in the first round and a 3–2 victory at home was
enough to see them through. In the second round they faced
Sparta of Prague and in the first (away) game Donald
MacKay suffered a pulled muscle. 'On you go, son,' was
Jerry Kerr's instruction to the young Hamish McAlpine, a
goalkeeper whose father had played for Dundee FC and
who had signed from North End some four years earlier.
The game was lost 3–1 and when only a 1–0 victory was
recorded at Tannadice the *Daily Record* attributed the
aggregate defeat to the substitution. More would be heard of
McAlpine, however.

In season 1970–71, Dundee FC fared much better. They
were in sixth place at the halfway mark (United were 13th
and this was also the season of the Ibrox disaster, when 66
people died and 103 were injured as railings collapsed on a
stairway at the end of the New Year Rangers–Celtic match)
and qualified for Europe in spite of yet another home defeat
from United. The Terrors were now unbeaten at Dens for
nine years, but changes were on the way, for McLean was
beginning to make his presence felt as a hard worker and
disciplinarian and, following a successful pre-season tour of
France and Belgium, Dundee FC began the 1971–72 season
brightly, including a long-awaited win over United at Dens.
The final score was 6–4 to the Dark Blues and McLean's
after-match comment was particularly revealing: 'At 5–1
up,' he said, 'we had a tremendous chance of a big win to

make up for all the years we couldn't beat United.' There is no doubt where his loyalties lay at this time and in the short time he was at Dens as coach his results spoke for themselves.

In the revamped Fairs Cup (1971–72) – the European Union or UEFA Cup – Dundee beat Academisk (Denmark) 4–2 (home) and 1–0 (away) in the first round. In the second round they faced their old rivals FC Cologne and although they lost 2–1 in Germany, a Duncan hat-trick saw them through 4–2 at Dens. Remarkably, they now drew AC Milan and once again the Italians proved to be the stumbling block. In Milan, Dundee lost 3–0 and in spite of a fantastic performance at Dens Park they went down 3–2 on aggregate (Wallace and Duncan scored at Dens). The Dundee FC team was: Hewitt; R. Wilson and Houston; Steele, Phillip and Stewart; Duncan, Lambie, Wallace, J. Scott and J. Wilson. 'Dundee Football Club,' said Jock Stein, 'played better against Milan than any other Scottish team, and that includes Celtic.' But even a tribute as eloquent as this could not produce a result and it is results (and clichés) which count in this game.

Some Scottish football clubs suddenly now appeared to wake up to a crisis and Dundee was one. Attendances had been steadily falling throughout football since the '50s but the respective figures for Dundee FC's campaigns in 1961 and 1971 say it all. In 1963 the game at Dens against AC Milan was watched by 40,000 spectators. The equivalent tie in 1971 drew only 15,000 and indeed the combined attendances for all three 1971 games just managed to pass the 40,000 mark. Tournaments such as the UEFA Cup and Texaco Cup were designed to provide mid-table clubs with attractive games, but the plan did not appear to be working and something had to give. Events in the footballing history of the City of Dundee now took a momentous turn.

On 11 November 1971 Dundee United had called a press

conference for the first time in their history to announce that Jerry Kerr – Scotland's longest-serving manager with 12½ years' service – had resigned as team manager to take up the position of general manager at the club. The seemingly indestructible Kerr had taken ill at a match against Hibs and it was obvious the barracking he was receiving from some fans as a result of United's poor start to the season was taking its toll. One of the candidates for the job was Davie White, the ex-Rangers manager who had been replaced at Ibrox by Willie Waddell, but before an appointment could be made the spotlight returned to Dens, where John Prentice also seemed poised to make a statement. Prentice's utterances following the first Milan game had been increasingly pessimistic ('What's the point?' 'What's the future of the game in Scotland?') and when his home in Barnhill was seen to be advertised for sale, it was obvious he planned to go. What happened next, however, would have taxed the imagination of a soap opera scriptwriter.

Chairman James Gellatly made the first move by accepting Prentice's resignation and announcing it to the press. Simultaneously he announced that Prentice's successor would be none other than Davie White and the fact that White had been a player under Prentice at Clyde suggests that he was recommended for the Dundee job by his former boss. Now this meant that Jim McLean as Dundee FC coach was overlooked for the manager's job and whether he expected this can only be gauged from the news the following day that the new United manager was – Jim McLean. Here was one man who was quite sure not only that football had a future, but that he was going to play a major part in it.[2]

'It could mean the start of a new era for the club,' said the *Courier* prophetically of United's new manager, and again it was emphasised that McLean would have full control of the playing side while Kerr looked after the administration. His first pool was McAlpine, Rolland, Mollison, J. Cameron, W. Smith, D. Smith, Markland, Henry Traynor, Copland, K. Cameron, Gordon and Reid (Ian Mitchell,[3] Billy Gray, Joe Watson and Morris Stevenson were injured) and his first post-match assessment following a 2–2 draw with Ayr United was: 'Not good enough.' It was a cry which would often be heard from the manager's office.

Jim Steele, Dundee's skilled, if somewhat agricultural midfield player, now went to Southampton for £80,000 – and later won an FA Cup-winners' medal;[4] Tommy Gemmell left Celtic for Nottingham Forest, and another fine club servant, Ronnie Yeats, left Liverpool for Tranmere Rovers. 'No player in the history of the Liverpool club,' said Bill Shankly, 'has given greater service than Yeats . . . he proved the very foundation of our tremendous success and I cannot pay him too great a tribute.'

The *Courier* also let slip something which might be regarded as a little biased when, in describing the United fans' heckling of Jim Steele, it remarked, 'The frustrating terracing "Arabs" mounted a continuing offensive.'[5]

How that kind of thing goes down in the Tannadice boardroom can best be described as a kind of conspiracy theory. But it did not put McLean off his stride for, having outlined his philosophy of 'winning, but winning well' and giving 'entertainment value', he got down to a veritable orgy of football management. The cornerstone of his managerial career was to be a youth policy – initially to bring down the average age of the team – and his first list of 'S' form signings makes interesting reading. Not only does it contain the name of David Narey (St Johns) but also that of Cameron Fraser (Linlathen). The youngsters, of course, required assistance from older players as well as from management and once again the value of men such as Doug Smith and Denis Gillespie was in evidence in the transitional period. But McLean also made some astute moves in the transfer market, selling Alan Gordon (to Hibs for £12,000) and buying George Fleming (from Hearts, £7,000), Pat Gardner (from Dunfermline, £4,500) and Archie Knox (from St Mirren, £3,000). Frank Kopel was then picked up as a free transfer from Blackburn Rovers and McLean's commendable desire to build from within the community was further underlined when he insisted that *all* players must live in Dundee and district.

Davie White was also getting some change at Dens Park, where Duncan, Wallace and Jocky Scott were linking up well, but 'on the ground' McLean was having it all his own way. Twenty-two young players, mostly locals, showed their paces at Tannadice in McLean's first six weeks, whereas most of Dundee's young signings came from other parts of the country. They did have one notable success, however, when in July 1972 an Edinburgh youngster named Gordon Strachan signed for Dundee FC on an 'S' form.[6]

Dundee FC finished fifth and United ninth at the end of the first four months under new management, but both clubs were attracting poor crowds and their problems were compounded by the growing presence of the 'football hooligan'. Often victims of unemployment or broken homes, young rowdies discovered they could bring attention to themselves by behaving violently at football matches. Dundee FC somehow managed to attract a particularly malevolent crew who chose to imitate the hooligan element of the Rangers support and sing Orange and Loyalist songs. This was particularly inappropriate because, as explained earlier, Dundee United had come into being in part to repudiate sectarianism; and many of the young Dundee fans were themselves Catholics, who now could be found in the Dens Road enclosure mindlessly singing 'No Surrender' and 'God Save the Queen'! Willie Waddell of Rangers spoke out against his 'unruly mobs' at this time, but to date no such public statement has been heard from a Dundee FC chairman.

Bobby Seith now became manager of Hearts; Peter Ustinov was reaching the end of his term as Rector of the University of Dundee; and Jim McLean picked up where Jerry Kerr had left off, beating Dundee 2–1 at Tannadice.

United now went to the top of the league and stayed there for seven games and their final position of seventh (1972–73) was a significant improvement for McLean's first season. Dundee FC, however, went two better (fifth place), partly due to the performance of Scotland's top goalscorer, John Duncan (40 goals); and when the young forward scored two against the English League, it became a question of *when* he would move to an English club rather than if. In fact, the transfer, to Tottenham Hotspur for £140,000, did not go through until October 1974, by which time United themselves had found a goalscoring ace and Duncan had helped Dundee FC win another trophy.

NOTES

1 United changed to an all-tangerine strip in 1969.

2 One casualty of the merry-go-round was Doug Cowie, who had been appointed coach to United in 1966. He would later be re-employed, however.

3 Ian Mitchell was transferred to Newcastle United in season 1969–70 for £50,000. He did not establish himself in the first team, however, and returned, just before McLean arrived, in exchange for Alec Reid.

4 Steele teamed up at Southampton with Jimmy Gabriel.

5 The 'Arabs' was a name given to United and their fans by their Dundee rivals when, in the harsh winter of 1963, they burned ice – and the grass – from their pitch and put down sand to make the surface playable.

6 Clubs were limited to 20 'S' signings, not more than ten in each age group 13–14 and 14–15.

SEVENTEEN

Andy Gray, a United 'S' form signing from Drumchapel, was the first young star to emerge from Jim McLean's galaxy. Capped by Scotland's schoolboys, juveniles, amateur youth and professional youth teams, the powerful young centre-forward was a terrific scoop for scout Maurice Friel[1] and was obviously won over by McLean's promise of an early chance of first-team football. He made his début against East Fife in August 1973 and teamed up alongside club stalwarts like Sandy Davie, who had returned from a spell in English football,[2] and Andy Rolland.

Graham Payne (St Columba's) was the next youth to be called into the first-team squad and McLean's policy contrasted sharply with that of White, who seemed to concentrate his efforts on the transfer market and even the free transfer market whence came Tommy Gemmell. In fairness, however, White put together a successful team more quickly than did McLean and at least one free-transfer man, goalkeeper Thompson Allan, was a great signing for the club. In the 1973 League Cup, Dundee FC qualified from Section 3, which included Hearts, St Johnstone and Partick Thistle. Defender Ian Phillip, who had gone to Crystal Palace the previous season for £112,000, returned to Dens for £60,000 and Dundee also tried to bring back Steve

Murray from Aberdeen. The side had acquired a certain rhythm and defeated Clyde 3–2 on aggregate in the next round. An experimental offside rule was used in the competition that year, but it had no effect on Tommy Gemmell's foraging style and one of his long-range specials against Kilmarnock put Dundee FC into the final.

The Scottish League Cup final played at Hampden Park on Saturday, 15 December 1973, took place in most peculiar circumstances. The country was in the middle of a fuel crisis which, compounded by an overtime ban by the miners and railwaymen, had led industry to the brink of a three-day week. In order to conserve power, the game between Dundee FC and Celtic kicked off early and with generators standing by. Further, it was snowing in the Glasgow area and this deterred a number of Dundee fans (attendance: 30,000). Happily for them it did not deter Gordon Wallace who, in the 75th minute, chested down a Bobby Wilson free kick in the penalty area and smacked it into the left-hand corner of the Celtic net. White did not think the game should have taken place, but was doubtless glad that it did. The Dundee FC team was: Allan; Wilson and Gemmell; Ford, Stewart and Phillip; Duncan, Robinson, Wallace, J. Scott and Lambie. Substitutes: Johnston and I. Scott.

The victory came as a great boost to Dundee FC who had lost their unbeaten European home record earlier in the season to FC Twente Entschede (1–3, 2–4 away) in the UEFA Cup, and United, too, received something of a morale boost with a couple of great aggregate victories against English opposition in the Texaco Cup. Sheffield United were dispatched in the first round (0–0 away, 2–0 home), Leicester City in the second (1–1 away, 1–0 home) and only an away disaster prevented them from overcoming Newcastle United in the third round (2–0 home, 1–4 away). Midfielder Jim Henry[3] was the architect of victory in these games and with Gray established in the first team, and

Narey, Payne and John Holt in the reserves, McLean was moved to comment: 'I firmly believe that here at Tannadice we have a group of youngsters that any manager north or south of the border would be proud to be connected with.'

Dundee FC began the year 1974 with a 2–1 victory over United at Tannadice and then embarked upon a remarkable Scottish Cup campaign which became known as their 'Month of Sundays', as their ties were played on Sundays that season. Aberdeen went down 2–0 at Pittodrie. Rangers (now managed by Jock Wallace) lost 3–0 at Ibrox and, following a 3–3 draw with Hibs at Easter Road in the fifth round, Dundee FC pulled 30,000 fans to the Wednesday replay at Dens. The fans were obviously still there if the attraction was right and when Dundee FC won 3–0, Jim McLean described them as 'the best team in Scotland'. Yet again, they failed to live up to it, going down 1–0 to Celtic in the semi-final.

Now, almost unnoticed in the light of Dundee's remarkable series of results, United too had reached the semis, beating Airdrie, Morton and Dunfermline in a replay; and in the semi-final replay, Andy Gray scored the winner in a 3–2 victory over Hearts (the first game was drawn 1–1). It was United's first 'real' Scottish Cup final and a great reward for servants like Doug Smith. The game was Sandy Davie's last for United before he emigrated and a great performance meant it was no fault of his that the Jute City missed out on a Cup 'double' that season. United were outplayed by Celtic and lost 3–0, but they did qualify for the European Cup-winners' Cup. The United team was: Davie; Gardner and Kopel; Copland, D. Smith and W. Smith; Payne, Knox, Gray, Fleming and Houston.[4] Substitutes: Traynor and Rolland.

The Terrors also had two unusual 'supporters' at the final: Dundee FC director Ian Gellatly, who claimed that Dundonians were all on the same side on such a day; and

Billy Connolly, the Scottish comedian who was beginning to break through in a big way in 1974 and who claimed divided loyalty because of the support he had received over the years from the Dundee Folk Club.

Meanwhile, the cost of Ninewells Hospital had soared to £24.5 million; the activities of ex-Provost Tom Moore, Bailie J.L. Stewart and Councillor Harry Dickson were coming under increasing scrutiny; and Murdoch Wallace jun., proprietor of the JM Ballroom, now also took over its traditional rival, the Palais, in South Tay Street. Dundee finished fifth in the league and United eighth; Willie Ormond had his finest hour at the World Cup in Germany when his Scotland team outplayed Brazil and failed to qualify from their section on goal average (Thomson Allan made the squad); David Narey began to establish himself in the United first team (as offers began coming in for Andy Gray); and another star was born when 16-year-old Paul Sturrock was named in the United first team pool in September 1974.

McLean was obviously warming to the task by now and appealed for bigger gates, which he said would enable him 'to bring honour to the city of Dundee'. In the Cup-Winners' Cup United beat Jiul Petrosani (Romania) in the first round 3–2 on aggregate, but went out 1–0 on aggregate to Bursapor after another long journey, this time to Turkey. Dundee went out of the UEFA Cup 5–2 on aggregate to RWD Amsterdam in the first round.

However, the clubs had quite a lot on their plates on the domestic front that year, for the much-discussed Premier League was to become a reality the following season (1975–76) and the ten-club Premier Division was to be composed of the top ten teams of the First Division. Again, White looked to the transfer market, bringing ex-United man Alan Gordon to Dens for £15,000. United did likewise, signing the 19-year-old Hamilton striker, Paul Hegarty, for

£40,000. United, as usual, however, also had youngsters coming through at the same time. Centre-forward David Dodds, for example, was a provisional signing by now and he would soon be followed by Derek Addison and Raymond Stewart. With United in fourth place in the league, McLean wisely used the 'safety net' of guaranteed Premier League status to introduce new young players.

Another young Dundonian, however, Robbie MacIntosh (24), drummer with the Average White Band, had his life cut tragically short when he was given heroin at a party in America, which the group was about to conquer.

NOTES

1 The former Dundee FC physiotherapist.

2 Donald MacKay was freed by Jim McLean and moved first to Southend United.

3 Henry, a local boy, later moved to Fulham, Aberdeen and Forfar. But for protracted illness, he might have done even better in the game.

4 Houston was the ex-Dundee FC player who had gone to Ibrox for £30,000, then come to Tannadice for £20,000. Jackie Copland was signed by Jerry Kerr from Stranraer for £10,000 in 1970. Walter Smith would later become McLean's right-hand man.

EIGHTEEN

The Scottish Premier League was inaugurated in 1975 and consisted of the following sides: Rangers, Hibs, Celtic, Dundee United, Aberdeen, Dundee FC, Ayr United, Hearts, St Johnstone and Motherwell. (This was the order in which the first ten clubs finished the previous season. The next 16 formed the First Division and the final 16 the Second Division.)

Neither Dundee FC nor United qualified for the League Cup, although Gordon Strachan made a notable breakthrough to the Dundee FC first team; Britain voted to join the Common Market; and East End Park, Dunfermline, sold the dearest pies in Scottish football (they were good, though, as I remember). Dundee FC captain Bobby Ford scored the first goal of the Premier League; and war was declared on football hooligans by Sports Minister Denis Howell. Once again, violence was not confined to a particular minority. Dundee's Lord Provost, for example, Mr Charles Farquhar, was charged with assault following an incident at Camperdown Golf Club in September 1975.

Andy Gray was transferred to Aston Villa for £110,000[1] – 'McLean must go' chanted the fans; Jocky Scott went to Aberdeen for £15,000; and McLean's master plan was taken a stage further as his young squad continued to pick up regular European experience.

In the first round of the UEFA Cup, United beat Keflavik of Iceland 2–0 (away) and 4–0 (home), but in the second round they went down 2–1 at home in the first game against FC Porto. 'They let the fans down,' said McLean and, indeed, this 'bad team' then put United out in a 3–2 aggregate. Tom McAdam was signed from Dumbarton for £40,000 in another attempt by McLean to find a finisher and this would be his problem position for some time before a solution was found from within the ranks.

At the turn of the year (1976), Dundee were seventh and United ninth out of ten; but whilst United gained ground, Dundee began to lose their position and on completion of their programme had 32 points from 36 games. Ayr United and Dundee United both had 31 points from 35 games and so, when the Ayr team beat Motherwell in a midweek game, it meant one of the Dundee clubs must go down following United's last match at Ibrox. In that game McAlpine took and missed a penalty but otherwise played well to gain a 0–0 draw. This meant it was Dundee FC which was relegated, for the first time in 38 years.

Relegation in 1976 marked the beginning of a nightmare for Dundee FC and Jim McLean was sympathetic. 'The penalty for failure is too great,' he complained and he favoured a 12-team division. McLean also said at a later date that the Premier League had come one season too early for United. It almost came too early for Aberdeen as well, for, as Dundee FC began to visit places like Hamilton and Montrose in the new season, United and Aberdeen – the two clubs which had finished directly above them – now raced to the top of the Premier League.

Doug Smith retired after 587 matches and no bookings – a fantastic record for a central defender at this time; Dundee FC, reckoning that relegation would cost them £100,000 per season, became agents for Rangers Pools; and Rangers themselves ran into another storm when their fans rioted during a game with Aston Villa. The following week Rangers general manager Willie Waddell declared that in future there would no longer be religious barriers at Ibrox – although for many years the actual number of Catholics signed could still be counted on one finger.[2] The next Saturday the Rangers fans stayed away in droves and those who did attend sang ditties like 'You can stick your Fenian players . . .' When Jock Wallace on his return to Ibrox in 1983 remarked that 'no one spoke about sectarianism when he was winning trebles' (Rangers won the treble in 1975–76), his memory failed him somewhat.

Another manager facing a problem was Jerry Kerr, who by this time had moved to Forfar Athletic with less than spectacular results. In what was an uncharacteristically distasteful episode, Kerr had been forced out at Tannadice in 1972 and failed to recover his touch after two years at Forfar (1974–76). He was succeeded at Forfar by Archie Knox and later worked with Dundee FC.

David Narey was now the lynch-pin of the United defence and Gordon Wallace had crossed the road to lead the Tangerine attack; punk rock had arrived and the Sex Pistols were banned from appearing at the Caird Hall; and Jimmy Carter was the new American President. Britain also had a new leader, for Harold Wilson, who had led his Labour Party to victory in 1974, now handed over the reins to Jim Callaghan; and football pundits on the west coast were also beginning to get a whiff of the wind of change as United and Aberdeen began to get results regularly on their territory.

Davie White, unfortunately, was not so lucky and resigned when he failed to get Dundee FC back into the Premier League in one season. His replacement was his League Cup-winning skipper – Tommy Gemmell – who for all his playing years had no coaching experience and did not apply for the job. The wisdom of the board's choice was soon to be tested.

One of Gemmell's ex-team-mates, Billy McNeill, now became manager of Aberdeen in succession to Ally MacLeod. Another, Jimmy Johnstone, signed up as a player with 'Big Tam' at Dens. The latter move was not a success, however, although Dundee began well with Gordon Strachan as captain. Over at Tannadice three more names were figuring on McLean's teamsheets, Ralph Milne and Derek Stark in the reserves, and Billy Kirkwood in the first team. Another Dundee FC player and cap, Bobby Robinson, crossed the road in exchange for Billy Williamson plus £20,000. Another striker, John Bourke, came to United from Dumbarton, while McAdam went to Celtic. And another rock star – this time one of the greatest, Elvis Presley – succumbed to the ravages of drugs. KB Copenhagen put United out of the UEFA Cup 3–1 on aggregate; McLean condemned drunken hooligans; and Dundee FC looked to have picked up two good youngsters in Ian Redford and the younger Ian Ferguson. The hope of rearing their own team like United, however, suffered a setback when Gemmell accepted a £50,000 bid plus Jim Shirra from Aberdeen for a young man who would go on to become one of the greatest players in the Scottish game – Gordon Strachan.

Liverpool, who had signed Kenny Dalglish from Celtic, watched Graham Payne, but he didn't go; Newcastle watched and bid for David Narey – he didn't go either; and Donald MacKay, the ex-United goalkeeper now at Bristol City as coach, was offered a similar position in Aslborg in Denmark. He didn't go.

Dundee FC failed again to get promotion (1978) and Scotland suffered their greatest humiliation in Argentina. One consolation for United at least was that three of their players – Narey, Hegarty and Payne – made the World Cup 40 and their third place in the Premier League put them comfortably into Europe again. Standard Liege, just as comfortably, put them out, unfortunately, but Jim McLean's 'education' was now nearing completion.

Billy McNeill became manager at Celtic and was replaced at Aberdeen by ex-St Mirren boss Alex Ferguson; Jock Stein went to Leeds United, then took on the Scotland job; and Jock Wallace, having won another treble, left Ibrox suddenly, proclaiming that he would never reveal the reason why. Perhaps the fact that the in-demand David Narey went to St John's Secondary School in Johnston Avenue had something to do with it.

NOTES

1 Gray had scored 40 goals in 96 games for United, and he would later be transferred to Wolves for a staggering £1.5 million. He was also the English players' Player of the Year in his first season with Aston Villa.

2 Rangers actually signed a Catholic in the 1950s and he was a Dundonian, Larry Blyth.

NINETEEN

David Narey, a central defender or midfield player and an outstanding, instinctive reader of the game, was the first Dundee United player to receive a full Scotland cap. When he played his first full game against Portugal in November 1978, the Lion Rampant was hoisted over Tannadice. The club topped the Premier League at the time and Dundee FC were top of the First Division, and although the Dark Blues looked to be geared towards promotion as an end in itself, they won their championship (1978–79) in an exciting climax and saved the club from financial disaster. Dundee FC from: Donaldson, Barr, Millar, Schaedler, Watson, Glennie, Shirra, Williamson, McLaren, Pirie, Sinclair, Murphy, Caldwell, McGhee, Redford and Lamb. Billy Pirie and Ian Redford were prolific goalscorers for the club.

Margaret Thatcher became Prime Minister and Gordon Wilson retained his seat in Dundee East for SNP, although his majority was cut by the Labour candidate, former UCS shop steward Jimmy Reid. United toured Japan and Hamish McAlpine was sent home prior to the 'Japan Cup final' in which United States went down 2–0 to Spurs; Jim McLean signed a new five-year contract despite another offer for his services, this time from Toronto Metros; and he then signed Willie Pettigrew, the Motherwell centre-forward, for

£100,000. McAlpine was suspended and temporarily replaced by Peter Bonetti, the ex-Chelsea goalkeeper[1] who had moved his family from London to Mull. But you can't keep a good man down and the differences were soon patched up.

Dundee's George Stewart (£37,000) followed clubmate Bobby Hutchinson (£20,000) to Hibs and, given that another £30,000 had been received from Sheffield United the previous year for young centre-half John McPhail, Dundee FC were continuing to do quite well in the transfer market. The players who remained, however, were not suitably prepared for the Premier League and the team went down again in 1980.

Season 1979–80, however, will be remembered by the citizens of Dundee for another reason. This was the year United won their first major trophy. The club did not begin very cleverly in the league, but in what was their seventh European campaign they had a good victory over Anderlecht in the first round of the UEFA Cup (0–0 home, 1–0 away, a Kopel 'super goal'). In the second round they met Diosgyori Miskolc of Romania – a club whose name no one could pronounce comfortably except Mary Marquis – and United were also uncomfortable on the park, losing 1–0 at home and 3–1 away. The club were now on the march, however, and in October 1979 they paid a record fee for Chelsea's Scottish midfielder, Eamonn Bannon. The money had regrettably come from the £400,000 transfer of 20-year-old full-back Raymond Stewart to West Ham, but the deal paid off almost immediately, for within a month United had reached the sponsored final of the Bell's League Cup where they met east coast neighbours Aberdeen.

Results in earlier rounds were: second round – Airdrie 2, United 1; United 2, Airdrie 0; third round – Queen's Park 0, United 3; United 2, Queen's Park 1; fourth round – United 0, Raith Rovers 0; Raith Rovers 0, United 1; semi-final – United 6, Hamilton 2.

The first game at Hampden was drawn 0–0 after extra time, but when the replay was scheduled for Dens Park, United's hopes were high. United fielded: McAlpine, Stark, Kopel, Phillip,[2] Hegarty, Narey, Bannon, Sturrock, Pettigrew, Holt and Kirkwood. Aberdeen lined up: Clark, Kennedy, Rougvie, McLeish, Garner, Miller, Strachan, Archibald, McGhee, McMaster and Scanlon. Payne was left on the bench owing to the heavy conditions, but second-half goals from Pettigrew (2) and Sturrock brought the trophy to Tannadice. For ex-chairman Ernest Robertson the wait had been some 54 years, but well worth it.[3] And for Aberdeen there was consolation when they won their first Premier League championship in 1980. The New Firm had arrived.

At Dens, however, there was gloom and despondency. Ian Redford was transferred to Rangers for £200,000 and Tommy Gemmell went the way of so many football managers. The club was facing real financial difficulty now, but as usual there was no shortage of applicants for the manager's job and this time it went to the amiable Donald MacKay, the ex-United goalkeeper. At least MacKay had some knowledge of organisation, having worked in England and Europe, and with coach Frank Upton installed as his assistant, the key word became 'discipline'.

The Dundee youth policy was overhauled and Ian Ferguson, Stuart McKimmie and Ray Stephen began to challenge for first-team places; Cammy Fraser (the same Cameron Fraser whom McLean had signed then released as a 16-year-old) was signed from Hearts for £60,000; and against all expectations Dundee FC made it to the 1980–81 League Cup final, beating Aberdeen over two legs in the semi. What would make this an even more special event, however, was that their opponents would be the holders, Dundee United, and the venue, on the toss of a coin, Dens Park.

On Saturday, 6 December 1980, the teams lined up.

Dundee FC: R. Geddes, Barr, Schaedler, Fraser, Glennie, McGeachie, Mackie, Stephen, Sinclair, Williamson and A. Geddes. United: McAlpine, Holt, Kopel, Phillip, Hegarty, Narey, Bannon, Payne, Pettigrew, Sturrock and Dodds.

On a cold day, the first half was evenly contested. Sturrock, however, did not receive the close attention he now required and just before half-time Dodds got on the end of one of his probing crosses to score. In the second half Dundee had a reasonable penalty claim turned down when McAlpine dived at the feet of Stephen – but it did not matter in the final analysis, because two late goals from Sturrock sealed Dundee's fate. The (restricted) attendance was 24,700.

Chairman Johnston Grant must have been very proud. But, remembering the dark, downtrodden days, he might have been excused for shaking his head when he learned that McLean now had to *ask* the civic authorities if the players could display the cup in the City Square, for no invitation had been forthcoming. The council claimed 'a slight hiccup in communications', but I'm sure the old conspiracy was suspected at Tannadice . . .

In Europe, United went out again to Lokeren of Belgium on the away goals rule, but McLean was not too downhearted. 'I feel we are now on the right road to success,' he said, and no wonder. Besides his Cup-winning players he had the prospect of still more brilliant youngsters to look forward to: Ralph Milne, for example, a winger whose speed and power promised great things (he had already scored a great goal at Parkhead); Richard Gough, a South African defender, recommended to the club by ex-Dundee stalwart Alec Hamilton; and Maurice Malpas, a cultured and intelligent left-side player.

In the United States events took something of a crazy turn when first John Lennon was shot dead by an obsessed maniac, and then the new President, Ronald Reagan, was wounded by another individual with the same obsession.

In Dundee, thankfully, things were slightly less crazy. Following on his League Cup achievement, MacKay brought the team back up in one season. Paul Sturrock, described by McLean as 'the country's most exciting player', was one of Scotland's top goalscorers, capped, and named Player of the Year. And United reached the final of the Scottish Cup (1981), although they lost 4–1 to Rangers in a replay. United: McAlpine, Holt, Kopel, Phillip, Hegarty, Narey, Bannon, Milne, Kirkwood, Sturrock and Dodds. Substitutes: Pettigrew and Stark.

* * *

Dundee United had arrived as a major force in Scottish football. But, although even greater things might be ahead of them on paper, no football fan, whether connected or unconnected with the club, will forget their performances in season 1981–82 and the European games in particular. As League Cup holders, United once again qualified for the UEFA Cup and in the first round they drew the French club AS Monaco. As the name suggests, this team came from that famous principality and indeed enjoyed the patronage of Prince Rainier and Princess Grace (Grace Kelly, the former film star).

> I remember the time it was an evening game
> A European tie in the howling rain.
> Gus Foye pointed to the side of the goal and said
> 'There's Grace Kelly by Taylor Brothers Coal'
> At Tannadice . . .
> – *Hamish the Goalkeeper* by Michael Marra

The first leg was played away and all of Europe got what the

French daily newspaper *Nice Matin* described as a 'surprise' when the Terrors ran up a 5–2 score. 'We did not think,' it continued, 'that AS Monaco could be beaten so emphatically by *anyone*.' However, there were no hard feelings; and as it tied in with the marriage of some of their aristocratic chums in Scotland, the return match at Tannadice was witnessed by the royals themselves. This attracted a number of people who would not normally go to Tannadice. When the home team lost 2–1, McLean was particularly displeased and fined his players. In a way this was understandable, for Mrs Thatcher's monetarist economic policies were deliberately creating unemployment (the UK figure was now 3 million) and money was scarce.

The team had an early opportunity to restore themselves in the second round when they drew the famous German side, Borussia Moenchengladbach. In the first (away) game the score was 2–0 for Borussia, but the following Wednesday United scored a brilliant 3–0 victory in the League Cup semi-final against Aberdeen. So by the time the European return game came along, the United players were ready to make up for their earlier misdemeanours. In a performance of breathtaking quality, they scored no less than five times without a reply and with a rare flash of humour McLean described it as 'nothing short of not bad'! Nine of the victorious team had been reared by the club and the other two (Bannon and Hegarty) cost only £200,000. United: McAlpine, Holt, Murray, Gough, Hegarty, Narey, Bannon, Milne, Kirkwood, Sturrock and Dodds.

In the League Cup final – United's third in succession – Stark replaced Murray and Phillip replaced Gough, and their opponents were Rangers. Milne scored in 49 minutes and three minutes later it looked all over when Sturrock crashed in a brilliant 35-yard drive. Holt, however, was adjudged to have been offside and the loss of two goals in the last 14 minutes meant the Cup was leaving Tannadice.

In Europe, though, they marched on, beating Winterslag of Belgium (0–0 away, 5–0 home). In the quarter-finals they were drawn against Radnicki of Yugoslavia. At Tannadice in March 1982 United won 2–0, but in return the Terrors 'froze' and went out 3–0 to what McLean rightly described as 'the worst team we have met in competition so far'.

NOTES

1 Former Arsenal star Charlie George also 'looked in' at Tannadice in 1982 but failed to make the first team.

2 Ian Phillip had moved from Dens to Tannadice.

3 Ernest Robertson died in January 1982.

TWENTY

Dundee Football Club finished eighth out of ten in season 1981–82, so Donald MacKay had done well in keeping them up, but the financial crisis would not go away and at an extraordinary general meeting of the club on 16 March 1982 their debt was so heavy they decided to 'go public' in an attempt to raise some capital; 430,000 ordinary shares of £1 were put on the market to be sold in blocks of £250 and the initiative raised £115,000 from public subscription. This compared with a trading loss of £297,000 for one year (ended 31 May 1982) and could only have made a small impression upon the overall debt, which was estimated by the press at around £500,000.

The modern Dundee Football Company, like the modern Dundee United Football Company and, indeed, like a large number of British companies, had its origins during the Second World War. The pre-war company, with James A. Galloway as chairman, David How as vice-chairman and William McIntosh still a major shareholder (Simpson retired in 1939, Galloway in 1944), went into mothballs in 1940 as the previous season's accounts had shown a loss of £1,400 and there were no prospects of the situation improving.

In 1944, 'Wattie' Simpson sold 500 shares to James

Gellatly and another director, Joseph Murray Wilkie, who was the solicitor appointed to sell the shares of Mr How (now deceased). These shares were distributed by Mr How in the following manner: 200 to himself on behalf of Mrs How; 490 to James R. Gellatly (CA); 900 to James Swadel (cooked meat manufacturer); 900 to Bailie John Thomson and 50 to A.P. McGill. Swadel and Thomson then sold 400 each to club managing director George Anderson; Gellatly sold his 490 to Anderson and when Andrew Clark joined the board in place of Galloway in 1945 it was constituted as follows: Bailie Thomson (chairman), James R. Gellatly, J. Swadel, F. Graham, A. Clark, J.M. Wilkie and G. Anderson, with R. Crichton as company secretary. Gellatly's firm of accountants took over the audit. Although the players and ex-players of Dundee FC and Dundee United continued to 'to and fro' between the clubs, the business at least was beginning to separate again and this process was completed on the death of William McIntosh in 1955.

McIntosh was something of a king-maker, for just as his shares in the United Company gave George Fox and Johnston Grant a firm foothold on the United board, so the distribution of his shares in the Dundee FC Company helped found the dynasty which was to control Dundee Football Club. Gellatly, Clark, Graham and Swadel each received 223, with 148 going to Robert Crichton, and when George Anderson died in 1956 the distribution of his shares confirmed the trend (Gellatly 520, Clark 255, Graham 255, Swadel 255).[1]

By the late '50s, therefore, James Gellatly with 1,958 shares was the principal shareholder in Dundee Football Club (other major shareholders were Graham 1,088, Thomson 1,513, Swadel 1,513 and Clark 900). By 1963, having guided them to a League championship, two League Cups, a Scottish Cup final and a European Cup semi-final, he was the most successful chairman in the history of the

club and one of the most successful provincial chairmen in
the history of Scottish football. By that time, however, he
also held 19 other directorships – including one of Reform
Properties[2] to which he transferred 1,600 shares in 1962 –
and had lost out to Dundee United in a crucial initiative in
the city, namely football pools. This would be one of the
factors which eventually tipped the footballing scales in
Dundee.

Taypools was begun in 1956 under the Pools Betting Act
of 1954. It was run privately by the Dundee United
Sportsmen's Club with the proceeds going to the football
club.[3] As stated earlier, when Johnston Grant and George
Fox joined the United board in 1955 under the chairmanship
of Ernest Robertson, the club was £10,000 in debt. By 1957
the proceeds of Taypools were responsible for the club
going into profit and by 1959 they were worth more than
£10,000 annually to Dundee United. This meant the
difference between profit and loss, development and
stagnation. It meant that the club, properly managed, could
now slowly build on the field.

Dundee FC, meanwhile, had success – colossal success –
which between 1959 and 1966 brought in a net £250,000 in
transfer fees alone. Such a sum of money should have
enabled them to mount a sustained and effective challenge
for honours in Scotland and Europe. But it didn't. It did not
even establish a scouting system capable of attracting the
cream of young Scottish talent; and in the case of Gordon
Strachan in the '70s, even when it did find talent, the club
appeared to lose the ability to transfer players at a sensible
price. What went wrong?

To my mind it was simply a question of style. Whereas
Jim McLean would demonstrate that one man with his feet
on the ground, by sheer hard graft and the imposition of
simple disciplines in respect of coaching, training and
scouting, could build a side of European quality from

moderate financial resources, Dundee FC – who had had the same man in their employ and let him go to their rivals – seemed to prefer big 'names' as managers and big business in the boardroom, when the size of the operation simply did not justify it. Further, companies were not required to disclose dividends paid to directors until 1968. In that year (and this was a few years after the 'good times'), from a profit of £11,961.16s.5d, Dundee FC paid a dividend of 25 per cent. In my view this is an extraordinarily high figure when something like 10 per cent is the norm, and probably less in the case of football clubs.

By then, housebuilding magnate John Bett had become a Dundee FC director and, frankly, with Reform Properties also a major shareholder, the board looked more like that of an estate agent than a football club. Symbolically, James R. Gellatly now moved house to the grounds of Castleroy – the former baronial home of the jute-owning Gilroy family in Broughty Ferry. Losses of £28,225 and £32,441 were sustained by Dundee Football Club in 1969 and 1971 respectively, with a small profit of £720 in 1970. In 1971 Mr I. Gellatly CA, son of James Gellatly, became a director and company secretary and 1972 and 1973 were both profitable years (£46,178 and £55,003). In a year which saw no substantial outgoing transfers, however – such as 1974 – the difficulties under which Dundee FC were trading were there for all to see. That year the loss was £93,436. Another increase in the share capital looked inevitable in 1977, with Ian Gellatly installed as chairman. By the creation of 60,000 £1 shares, the share capital of the club became £70,000; of the 70,000 shares, the more substantial holdings of directors and their families, and others, were Ian Gellatly (25,356), Ian Bett (3,500), Albert Bett (3,000),[4] Graham Thomson (5,507) and William Lyburn (5,507).

These people were at least putting their money where their mouths were, but once again, when one considers the shares held by Reform Properties (12,392) and Inverblair (5,000), the impression persists of businessmen locked in a game of Monopoly rather than football persists. And they did not appear to be winning that game either, for losses continued unabated: 1976 (£5,468); 1977 (£56,458); 1978 (£47,682); 1979 (£55, 456). One bright spot was that the Dundee FC Sportsmen's Club was now managing to contribute more substantial sums of money (£14,000 in 1976; £28,000 in 1977; £26,000 in 1978), but Taypools by comparison were handing over sums of around £50,000 in these years.

Ironically, whilst Dundee FC headed inexorably towards a public quotation, Dundee United decided to change their Articles of Association and become a private company (1972). Shares could no longer be sold among private individuals, but had to be offered first to the directors of the club. Given the experience of Dundee FC in this area, I am not certain of the wisdom of such a move, but at least their policy of promoting ex-players to the board was maintained: first Jim McLean, then Doug Smith received directorships in the early 1980s.[5]

In 1982, a life-long fan, Andrew Marshall, a caravan park operator from Cupar, became a director of Dundee FC by virtue of a £25,000 investment; Dundee FC became agents for Rangers Pools; and Bob Shankly and Billy Steel died in the same week.

NOTES

1 McIntosh's shares were distributed this way as they had to be offered to the board first. More significant, however, was the distribution of the shares of the 'jute barons' – Simpson, How, Galloway and Graham. It was therefore jute money which bought power in the club.

2 Directors (1981) Ronald Gellatly, Ian Gellatly and James. A. Gellatly.

ACROSS THE GREAT DIVIDE

3 Ernest Robertson originally loaned the money to finance Taypools.

4 John Bett died 1974. Neither I. Bett nor A. Bett was a director in 1977. James. A. Gellatly died 1978.

5 Leading Dundee United shareholders (1983) were George Fox (2,060), Johnston Grant (2,060), George Grant (1,630) and J. McConnachie (1,500). J. McLean held 997, J. Littlejohn 200 and D. Smith 97.

TWENTY-ONE

United began season 1982–83 with the signing of
Dundonian Ian Britton, a forward who had enjoyed success
with Chelsea, and the club was quoted as fourth favourite
for the Premier League, at 21–1. In the UEFA Cup they met
the crack Dutch side PSV Eindhoven and in the first game
at Tannadice the score was 1–1. Once again an intermediate
result against Aberdeen (this time 3–1 in the League Cup
quarter-final) provided a tonic and the away European game
was then won magnificently by two goals to nil.

Hamish McAlpine was capped as an over-age player by
the Scottish Under-21 team and in the second round of the
UEFA Cup he and his mates outclassed Viking of Stavanger
in Norway (3–1 away, 0–0 home). In the third round the
German team Werder Bremen was beaten 2–1 at Tannadice
and United survived a terrible pounding away from home to
secure a 3–2 aggregate win; but with Aberdeen also going
well in the Cup-Winners' Cup, it was generally felt that one
or both might land a trophy that year.

In the event it was Ferguson's Dons who did, beating
Bayern Munich in the semi-final and Real Madrid in the final,
for United were to go out again in the quarter-finals of their
tournament, to Bohemians of Prague. They managed to get a
good result in Czechoslovakia, going down 1–0, but at

Tannadice their goalscoring flair deserted them, so a European semi-final remained a dream. In the league, however, their creative style was pulling in the fans from all over the country and by New Year 1983 they were in second place to Celtic. The Glasgow side had 27 points from 15 games, United had 24 points from 15. Dundee FC, who were enjoying some great performances from Cammy Fraser and Ian Ferguson, were in fifth place. The holiday period was a significant time for all three clubs. United utterly dominated Dundee in the derby match, but then lost to Aberdeen, while the Dark Blues went on to Parkhead and won a point in a game which marked the beginning of a slide for Celtic.

The Timex factory was on strike over 1,900 projected redundancies and Clive Sinclair threatened to take his electronics business elsewhere; but the workforce 'sat in', for they had recently seen the Robb Caledon shipbuilding workers put out of a job and they were not about to follow suit. In the Scottish Cup it took a last-minute goal by Dundee FC to defeat Brora Rangers at Dens and United went out 1–0 away to St Mirren. But their neighbours had gone down in the Cup to the Buddies and by the same margin, in their championship year, so perhaps this was an omen. Again, Kilmarnock felt the Terrors' wrath, going down heavily for the second time that season, and with Maurice Malpas now a 'regular' alongside Gough, the team looked to have a better balance as time went on. Dundee FC were again defeated at Tannadice and although the Bohemians' result came as a blow to McLean, his remarks suggested that he still felt as though United could win the league. Again it was a result at Pittodrie which provided the boost when two Ralph Milne goals caught Bayern's conquerors on the hop. And again Dundee did them a good turn by beating Celtic 2–1 at Dens.

The positions were now as follows: Aberdeen played 25, points 42; United played 27, points 41; Celtic played 26, points 41. So the league was wide open, but United still had to visit Parkhead twice and the first (Wednesday) game was won 2–0 by Celtic. By now, however, United had five players in the Scotland squad as well as the assistant manager, so confidence was not the problem it had been in previous decades; and when the second Celtic match came along on Wednesday, 20 April 1983, they were able to put the first result behind them for what was a virtual league decider, given that Aberdeen had also lost points.

The atmosphere at Parkhead was electric and United twice took the lead through Hegarty and Bannon (penalty). Twice they were pulled back, however, and when Gough was ordered off in 58 minutes for becoming unnecessarily involved with Provan, it looked as though their chance had gone. It was at this point that Ralph Milne took a hand in things. Late in the game he controlled a cross from the right and coolly lobbed it over Bonnar in the Celtic goal. 'Now you're gonna believe us,' sang the United contingent. 'We're gonna win the league.' The Celtic support laughed, like a boxer who had taken a good punch but wanted to unnerve his opponent. The points, however, went to United.

With four games remaining, the Tangerines had to play Kilmarnock (home), Morton (away), Motherwell (home) and Dundee (away). Celtic still had a one-point advantage at this stage but Aberdeen, who were equal on points, beat the Bhoys 1–0 in the next game. United, meanwhile, beat Kilmarnock 4–0 and, in order to take full advantage of their pole position, the board hit on an ingenious scheme to give free admission vouchers to fans travelling to Greenock for the Morton game – thereby ensuring a large support. McAlpine had to go off injured in this game, but Hegarty was a more-than-capable deputy and United won 4–0.

Aberdeen, still equal on points with United, beat Dundee at Dens, but then dropped a point to Hibs, so when United beat Motherwell 4–0 in the penultimate game, the City of

Dundee was set for a spectacular league decider on Saturday, 12 May 1983. Dundee FC v Dundee United. Once again the soap opera scriptwriter[1] could not have dreamed up a better finale and at least Dundee FC were out of relegation trouble (they finished sixth). Dundee FC lined up: Kelly, Glennie, McKimmie, Fraser, Smith, MacDonald, Ferguson, McGeachie, Sinclair, Stephen and Kidd. Substitutes: Mackie, Scrymgeour. The Dundee United team was: McAlpine, Stark, Malpas, Gough, Narey, Hegarty, Bannon, Milne, Kirkwood, Sturrock and Dodds. Substitutes: Holt, Reilly.

In the opening minutes, when a gifted player will often try something extraordinary, Ralph Milne picked up a ball in the middle of the Dundee FC half and, seeing Kelly off his line, produced a chip goal from nothing. Kelly later made amends by saving a Bannon penalty. But the ex-Hearts and Chelsea player followed up to score and, although Ferguson pulled one back, in 25 minutes, 2–1 was United's league-winning margin.[2]

Although the club had used 15 players in the course of the season, it was a basic 12 players – the winning team, plus Holt – who carried the burden and McLean was quick to point this out during the post-match reception. He was, however, 'over the moon' and with St Johnstone winning the First Division and Brechin City the Second, Tayside was Scotland's Champion Region.

NOTES

1 James A. Michener, the popular American author of *Centennial*, received part of his education at St Andrews University in the early 1930s. In his book *On Sport* he reveals that during that time he was 'a most loyal partisan of Dundee United, in those days the nothing team of the League'.

2 Dundee United's league record for 1982–83 was: played 36, won 24, lost 4, drawn 8, goals for 90, goals against 35, points 56.

TWENTY-TWO

The Premier League flag was unfurled at Tannadice on a
sunny 20 August 1983, although no TV cameras were there
to record the event, owing to an industrial dispute. United
demolished Motherwell in the game which followed and
Jock Wallace, who had returned from Leicester City to the
Lanarkshire club, was fulsome in his praise of their
performance. Celtic, meanwhile, had transferred Charlie
Nicholas to Arsenal in the close season and were rumoured
to be interested in Paul Sturrock, but the United man was
injured in any case and the absence of these two strikers
gave Aberdeen something of a head start in the league.

Gordon Wallace left Raith Rovers to take up a coaching
position at Tannadice and Dodds was capped against
Uruguay, but things remained fairly low-key for the club
until Hamrun of Malta were dispatched in the first round of
the European Cup (3–0 away, 3–0 home). In the second
round United faced the Belgian champions Standard Liege
and, considering they were still without Sturrock, got a good
0–0 result away from home in the first leg. Instead of being
held up as an example of a fine footballing side, however,
United (and every other Scottish club) were relegated to
small print by the Scottish press as Rangers went through
yet another managerial trauma.

This time John Greig was for the axe – he had succeeded Jock Wallace in 1978 – and Alex Ferguson, who was the Ibrox board's first choice to replace him, turned the job down. The diversion suited McLean in a way, as he was quietly tuning his players up for the return game with Standard, and once again they responded with a magnificent 4–0 home victory. 'Bring on Liverpool,' chanted the fans and it was known that McLean did indeed fancy a shot at the English champs. But suddenly it was the turn of the United fans to suffer trauma when it was learned that Rangers had now decided McLean was the man they wanted as manager.

In spite of the fact that a reported £5,000 salary was on offer, plus perks and a free hand to sign anyone he wanted – irrespective of religion – it was with disbelief that the United support watched their hero visit Ibrox for talks with the Rangers chairman. Disbelief soon turned to joy, however, for after some deliberation, McLean decided against moving and to stay with United. 'No one,' said Patrick Barclay of *The Guardian*, 'could accuse Rangers of being trendy,' but at least they suited Jock Wallace, who now returned to his old stamping ground.

Ironically, on the Saturday before the talks (5 November 1983), a Peter Mackie goal had given Donald MacKay his first victory over United since he became manager and for the first time in quite a while Dundee FC seemed to be making progress. There was even talk of Europe again. The irony lay in the fact that one month later it was not McLean but MacKay who was on the move, resigning when the club accepted a £90,000 offer for Stuart McKimmie from Aberdeen and failed to buy replacements. His successor was Archie Knox, a man who had been McLean's first 'real' signing at Tannadice and until now assistant to Alex Ferguson at Pittodrie. Was he the man to change Dundee's fortunes? Many people in the game certainly thought so.

Meanwhile, back at Tannadice, United had paid £60,000

for one of Clydebank's young strikers, Tommy Coyne; the club were drawn against Rapid Vienna in the quarter-final of the European Cup; and Paul Sturrock pulled a shoulder muscle tying a shoelace! It was not to be his year for fitness. His team-mates were doing reasonably well in the league, however (third; Dundee FC eighth) and also in the League Cup, in the semi-final of which they now met Rangers. This tournament had not been much of a success that year – the *Glasgow Herald* suggested sponsorship might come from the Samaritans – and it further soured for United when, following a home draw, McLean got himself into trouble with the SFA for suggesting that too many of his team's games were being handled by west coast officials. Be that as it may, Rangers won the second leg 2–0.

The real stuff was in Europe, however, and in the first (away) game against Rapid, Derek Stark scored a vital goal in 30 minutes. United unfortunately lost two late goals, but McLean personally thought it was the finest performance he had ever seen from Hamish McAlpine and believed the result to be good enough. The Rapid coach, Otto Barie, did not agree, claiming that the Austrians would go through as they were 'streets ahead' of United; but, as Paul Sturrock remarked, the last man to say that was the Borussia coach. It was Sturrock's judgement which proved to be correct.

Archie Knox had a rather indifferent start at Dens, but his team performed well in the Scottish Cup and never better than in the quarter-final against Rangers. The first game ended in controversy when a 'good' score by Walker McCall was chalked off and it took a brilliant late strike from Albert Kidd to secure a replay.[1]

In the return at Ibrox, Fraser and Ferguson in particular struck a fine game and Dundee beat the 'Gers 3–2. In time-honoured fashion Rangers then signed these two players at the end of the season (1984), thus leaving Knox with something of an uphill struggle; but in any event Dundee FC went out to Aberdeen in the Scottish Cup semi-final and escaped relegation, finishing in eighth place. Knox was quoted as saying that it would take him eight years to put things right at Dens Park.

Before the return match with Rapid Vienna, McLean reminded his players of how they had been written off by the Austrian coach and the ploy worked, for in 21 minutes, Stark mishit a Gough cross and Dodds first-timed the ball into the net with a left-foot shot on the turn. This was enough to give United victory on the away goals rule.

The semi-final of the 1983–84 European Cup was contested by Liverpool, AS Roma, Dinamo Bucharest and Dundee United – again something which speaks for itself – and United drew the Romans with the first game at home[2] Now the final was also to be played in Roma's stadium, so McLean felt that the draw improved his team's chances of actually winning the competition. But his opinion was not shared by the 'intellectual' football correspondent of the *Sunday Times*. In what was probably the first article he had ever written about Dundee United – indeed, it was probably the first time he had ever *thought* about Dundee United – the supercilious Brian Glanville dismissed them as a 'biff-and-bang' side whose tactics would not trouble Roma. How anyone could describe a team which contained Maurice Malpas, David Narey, Eamonn Bannon, Ralph Milne and Paul Sturrock as playing 'up-and-at-'em' football is a mystery, but Glanville noticeably gave the subject a body swerve on Sunday, 15 April, for by then United were ahead by two goals to nil.

Roma, of course, were a great side. Coached by Nils Liedholm who, strangely enough, had also worked for AC Milan in 1963, they were a rich club who had spent their money on some brilliant players such as Brazilian Roberto Falcao and the Italian World Cup star Bruno Conti. Falcao in particular was the man who made the team tick. When he missed the first leg at Tannadice through injury, United took full advantage, scoring through Dodds in 48 minutes and Stark in 60. Almost unbelievably, United could have had more, for that 12-minute spell shook the Italians' confidence and both Milne and Hegarty came near. The game finished 2–0, however, and again McLean thought it was enough.

In the league he was not deriving the same satisfaction, for in a game against Dundee FC he again clashed with referee Alan Ferguson and, following the Roma match, Aberdeen ended his championship hopes for that year. The former incident was to have particularly unpleasant personal consequences for the United manager because, later in the season, he was fined by the SFA and banned from the touchline for a year – a decision which would cost him his assistant managership of the Scotland team.

In Rome it was death or glory. The return game was played in the suitably gladiatorial Olympic Stadium and watched by 68,060 people who paid £600,000 for the privilege – a record for an Italian club match. United lined up: McAlpine, Stark, Malpas, Gough, Hegarty, Narey, Bannon, Milne, Kirkwood, Sturrock and Dodds. The game kicked off at 3 p.m. and at two minutes past three United were given formal notice of the task in hand when Conti put the ball in the net. The 'goal' was chalked off, but this was the point of no return for United. Gamely, they tried to take the match to Roma and in 20 minutes almost scored when Dodds' brave dive for a Bannon cross gave Milne a chance. He steadied in front of the open goal, but the shot went over the bar and that, as they say, was that. Pruzzo scored in 21 minutes with a header and in 38 minutes with a shot, and in the second half a Di Bartolomi penalty ended United's dream. Everyone – including McLean, who was shamefully harassed by the Italian players at the end – admitted that the better side had won. But it once more fell to Glanville to scrape the bottom of the barrel. 'Poor, limp, mediocre

Dundee United' was one description and 'naïve' another.

Well, by Italian, English or even Scottish standards, United are not a rich club. The players did not give one of their best performances in Rome. But for a football club to come from the bottom four of the Scottish Second Division to the top four of Europe; from a wee, wooden stand built before the First World War, to the Olympic Stadium in Rome; to do this in 25 years, breaking, as they did, the century-old domination of Scottish football by the Old Firm along the way – the achievements of Dundee United in my opinion are without parallel in club football.

One more thing. Brian Glanville also described them in a kind of literary joke as 'plebeians'. Little did he know that in so doing he was echoing the stated ambition of one of the founding fathers of Dundee United Football Club, namely, to make them 'the people's club'.[3]

NOTES

1 McCall was a former Ayr United and Aberdeen player who had come to Dundee via Hong Kong. Albert Kidd, a Dundonian, cost MacKay a record £80,000 when he was transferred from Motherwell.

2 The home game, to the month, celebrated United's 75th anniversary – or to be more accurate, it was 75 years since the birth of Dundee Hibs.

3 Johnston Grant died in July 1984. He was widely regarded as the 'father' of the modern Dundee United.

CONCLUSION 1984

Although I was aware, even as a child in the '50s, that Dundee United were a poorer club financially than Dundee FC, it was much later that I heard United described as the 'working-man's team' – the implication being that Dundee FC somehow are not. Now this, to anyone who has seen the broad composition of the Dark Blues support, is plainly nonsense, for the vast majority of their fans come from the working classes and are indistinguishable from those of United. Yet the idea persists that Dundee FC consider themselves to be a better 'class' of club than United, who apparently must remain the poor relations in spite of their superior results and financial performance over the last ten years.

United have equalled Dundee in every respect (except the winning of the Scottish Cup, and Dundee's success was 75 years ago) yet when they (United) were invited to a nationally sponsored exhibition of Scottish football memorabilia in Dundee in 1983, their invitation came on the back of a facsimile of a cigarette card depicting a Dundee FC player. Is it any wonder they declined, or that their mild media paranoia intensified?

How did such attitudes arise? If we look at the historical facts we find that although Dundee are technically the older club, it can be argued that Tannadice Park is the older ground, football having been played on Clepington Park some 20 years before a ball was kicked at Dens. And since the principal forebears of both clubs, Our Boys and Harp, saw the light of day at approximately the same time, it is perhaps the superior playing record of Harp in the 1880s upon which attention should be focused rather than the grand delusions of Our Boys, who apparently looked down their noses even at their partners, East End.

It was the Dundee FC amalgamation, however, which seized the commercial initiative and from the 1890s onwards there is no doubt that the Dark Blues were the big Dundee club. For the next 30 years professional football in the city and Dundee Football Club were synonymous. There is also no doubt, however, that the body of men who founded Dundee FC in 1893 and rebuilt it at the turn of the century were ordinary working people – and the same was true of Pat Reilly's Dundee Hibs.

The clubs appear to have been closest in terms of their status, support and ambitions in 1925 when the reconstituted Hibs, Dundee United, prepared to enter the First Division. This was a time of great hope at Tannadice and, had things gone according to plan, they would soon have had a stadium to match the new Dens Park and a team to do it justice. But it was not to be. Of course, in the midst of the social turmoil of the time, even the well-laid plans of William McIntosh – that pillar of the Dundee Football Club establishment – went slightly agley and the complexity of the new situation as it developed over the next 30 years is perhaps best exemplified by the career of the Dundee FC and SFA treasurer. McIntosh was a hard-working and popular official with both the players and the fans who could readily give him a piece of their mind over the counter at the Opera Bar. He badly overstepped himself by opposing the advancement of Hibs and even their choice of name –

thus causing a great deal of ill-feeling amongst the Hibs' fans whose Irish ancestry had taught them a great deal about the misuse of power – and yet, ironically, it was McIntosh himself who, ten years later, was to feel the Iron Heel. For although Dundee FC had a grand new stadium, it still had to be paid for, and if the club was not enjoying success on the park their money would have to be found from a source other than their supporters. And where was there money in Dundee? In jute. Or to be more precise, in the hands of a small number of 'jute barons', mill owners, merchants and the like.

McIntosh now proceeded to encourage a number of them – Simpson, How, Galloway and Graham – to involve themselves in the affairs of Dundee Football Club and, looking upon it as just another business investment, they responded in the only way such people know how: by climbing to power, then kicking the ladder away. Willie McIntosh was duly forced out and how poetic it was that the main beneficiaries of Dundee FC's most crucial power struggle should be their greatest rivals, Dundee United. For at the bottom line, it was *football* which really interested McIntosh. Having swallowed his pride and crossed the road: (i) his administrative experience would have been invaluable to a small club with a cash crisis of its own; and (ii) his bitter experience at Dens would have given him the resolve to make sure that United did not similarly fall into the clutches of the capitalists. 'Ownership means control' and 'stay small think big' might have been his guiding principles at Tannadice and this approach has served the club well.

The way things turned out, of course, could not have been better written by James Michener – that aficionado of Dundee football himself – for while United regrouped around a board which included people who actually knew something about football (i.e. ex-players) and consolidated their support among the ancestors of immigrant jute *workers*, Dundee FC were stuck with power in the hands of jute *owners* and their appointed heirs. In a sense, *their* fans might have known what to expect and, surely, this was the time when the 'image' of the Dundee clubs was cast.

Image, however, is not everything and whilst the inevitability of the historical process was never more in evidence than in the professional football arenas of the city of Dundee over the last 30 or, indeed, 100 years, there is always the potential for change *if the lessons of history are learned*. For while United now constitute themselves on a private basis, the shares of Dundee FC are once again available to the general public (albeit at a price), so who knows what might happen? The fact that many people *care* suggests that the game, at least, is in good hands. Football is not 'just another business'. Here's to the next hundred years.

TWENTY-THREE

Whereas it might be said that Dundee FC peaked when they reached their 1963 European Cup semi-final, by 1984 United's golden climb had not yet reached its pinnacle.

Curiously, Dundee FC were also in fairly rude health in the mid-1980s and, following on from Donald MacKay, first Archie Knox then Jocky Scott would improve on their 8th position of 1984, to achieve 6th in 1985, 1986 and 1987 – thus narrowly failing to qualify for Europe on three consecutive occasions. This they did by some shrewd buying and selling: Cammy Fraser and Iain Ferguson to Rangers; John Brown, Bobby Connor, Stuart Rafferty and Tom Carson from the lower divisions. Knox and Scott were also able to enforce stricter discipline upon the team and it brought a rare win at Tannadice in the first derby of the 1984–85 season.

United, however, were unstoppable during this period. With George Fox succeeding Johnston Grant as chairman, McLean carried the club to another League Cup final (which they narrowly lost to an Iain Ferguson goal for Rangers) and then to an impossibly glamorous UEFA cup tie against Manchester United.

Dundee United had beaten AIK Stockholm in the first round (3–1 on aggregate) and Linz of Austria (7–2) and such was the breadth of their experience, a visit to Old

Trafford was not feared, but relished. Manchester United did, in fact, dominate the first game, but United came twice from behind for a 2–2 result which McLean felt on a par with the Terrors' breathtaking victory in Monaco. Back at Tannadice, however, the tangerine United could not impose themselves on a physical (and gifted) Reds side and they lost the home tie 3–2. Their season was not over, however, and a blistering Scottish Cup run took them to a final against Celtic in which they scored first, through Stuart Beedie. Late goals from Provan and McGarvey, however, once again kept United away from what was proving to be their most elusive piece of Scottish silverware.

The football season ended catastrophically, with 40 people dying as a result of crowd trouble at the Heysel Stadium in Brussels, prior to a Liverpool v Juventus European Cup final. And another 53 deaths occurred at Bradford City's Valley Parade ground when fire ripped through the old wooden grandstand in a period of a few minutes. (The Dens Park grandstand would also suffer fire damage around this time as a result of brainless, teenage arson.)

The early part of season 1985–86 was also marred by death, this time that of the great Jock Stein. The 'immortal' Celt (in Bill Shankly's famous words) had taken Scotland to the brink of qualification for the World Cup in Mexico when he collapsed and died of a heart attack at Ninian Park, Cardiff. Jim McLean had previously been the Big Man's assistant in the Scotland job and he now seemed to be inspired to achieve even greater things for his club.

The UEFA campaign that year stalled against Neuchatel Xamax of Switzerland, following victories against Bohemians of Dublin and Vardar Skopje from Yugoslavia. But United managed to supply five players for Alex Ferguson's Scotland squad in Mexico – Sturrock, Narey, Malpas, Bannon and Gough – so there was little doubt that the quality players were still in place for a European challenge.

At home, Dundee FC had brought a magnificent Hearts' season to a cruel conclusion with a last-game defeat at Dens Park; Archie Knox had decided to return to Pittodrie leaving Jocky Scott in charge; and Graeme Souness had come to Ibrox as player-manager with revolution on his mind. One of his first moves was to bring in Walter Smith as his assistant, but he failed to buy Richard Gough, McLean's policy of not selling to rivals sending the big defender to Tottenham Hotspur. Two fine players also travelled in the opposite direction: Dave Bowman and Jim McInally from Coventry City. Iain Ferguson returned to Dens on loan prior to a United bid which took the Ranger to Tannadice, and United's 1986–87 UEFA campaign kicked off with an aggregate victory over the French club, Lens (2–1). The next two rounds saw victories against Universitatea Craiova of Romania (3–1) and Hajduk Split of Croatia (2–0).

Graham Thomson succeeded Ian Gellatly at Dens in what would be a fairly short chairmanship but there was really only one game in town and it was United's third-round encounter with the mighty Barcelona whom they had defeated in both legs of a Fairs Cup match in 1966. The Catalan side had its predictable quota of stars – Gary Lineker, Bernt Schuster, Mark Hughes – but history was to repeat itself. United stormed to victory, 1–0 at Tannadice with a goal from United's new, young star Kevin Gallacher – his first in Europe – and 2–1 in Barcelona (Sturrock and Redford).

Next up were some more old (and vanquished) foes, Borussia Moenchengladbach, and the home result (0–0) gave Billy Thomson, who had now replaced Hamish in the United goal, his fifth clean sheet at home in the competition. In Germany, goals from the lethal Ferguson and Redford put the Terrors into the final.

For McLean, the big problem was raising his physically exhausted side for not one, but three big matches, because United had also reached the Scottish Cup Final, having beaten Dundee FC in the semis. IFK Gothenberg won the UEFA first leg 1–0 in Sweden, and a tired United failed to raise their game at Hampden against a St Mirren side managed by Alex Smith, with Saints' Ian Ferguson scoring the winner in extra time.

Everything now rested on the Gothenburg return and on Wednesday, 20 May 1986, although they failed to defeat the Swedes, Dundee United had their finest hour. Some of it came on the park – John Clark equalising a Nilsson strike – but the most memorable moments belonged to the fans who had the good grace to applaud a Swedish victory and celebrate the victory lap of honour. Their performance would earn United the respect of the entire football world and a special European football Fair Play award. United lined up: Thomson, Holt, Malpas, McInally, Clark, Narey Ferguson, Gallacher, Kirkwood, Sturrock and Redford. Substitutes: Bowman, Bannon, Beaumont, Hegarty and S. Thomson.

TWENTY-FOUR

Back at Dens, there was action both on and off the park. Dundee FC had transferred one of their stars, Bobby Connor, to Aberdeen; but Archie Knox had previously signed defender Jim Duffy, and Jocky Scott brought off a useful double, bringing in strikers Tommy Coyne from United (£75,000) and Keith Wright from Raith Rovers (£50,000). In the boardroom, property developer Angus Cook took control, buying shares from Gellatly and Ian Bett. There was some opposition to the idea of one man controlling the club but – following Wallace Mercer's lead at Hearts and with David Murray soon to take the helm at Rangers, then Fergus McCann at Celtic – Cook was merely in step with the times.

Jim Duffy now suffered a career-threatening injury at Ibrox and took up a coaching position at Dens. The situation looked healthier than for some time, but the game was moving very quickly in commercial terms with Souness adding weekly to his highly paid Rangers squad. Richard Gough joined from Spurs for £1.5 million to line up alongside Chris Woods, Terry Butcher, Graham Roberts, Mark Walters and the rest. John Brown had joined from Dundee FC and even the veteran Andy Gray was in the club's sights. Donald MacKay, meanwhile, had gone from Rangers reserve coach to manager of Blackburn, where he would team up again with Colin Hendry; and Jimmy Bone became coach alongside Gordon Wallace at Tannadice. United reached the Scottish Cup final once again in 1988 and this was the centenary event. But it proved no more fortunate for the Arabs, who again scored first through Gallacher but again lost two late goals, scored by Frank McAvennie.

Ian Porterfield, who had been Alex Ferguson's replacement at Aberdeen, resigned under something of a cloud and was replaced by Alex Smith who had been sacked by St Mirren (Ferguson had gone to Manchester United). Much to the consternation of Dundee FC fans, Smith was now joined at Pittodrie by Jocky Scott, who believed that he was not in Cook's long-term plans, and Drew Jarvie.

Even more surprising, however, was Scott's replacement at Dens. The virtually unknown Dave Smith was originally from Dundee and had been manager of Plymouth Argyle but, given the recent Porterfield experience, this was something of a gamble by Angus Cook. Everything is easier with hindsight, but Smith's term was truly disastrous for the Dark Blues and the club would lose much hard-won ground as a result. He only lasted 217 days and his replacement was another surprise – United coach Gordon Wallace – who immediately completed some great business for his new club, first by getting £500,000 for Tommy Coyne from Celtic and then by replacing him with a young Scot from Chelsea, Billy Dodds (£75,000).

At Tannadice, however, there was trouble at t'mill. Following a Scottish Cup semi-final incident with Willie Miller, Jim McLean had been rather savagely fined £6,700 and banned from the touchline for three years. His threatened resignation was then overtaken by an incident at Edinburgh Airport when he head-butted a BBC cameraman; and, to complete something of boardroom nightmare, George Grant, brother of Johnston and replacement chairman for George Fox, died after two days in the job. On 20 December 1988, James Y. McLean, manager of Dundee United, also became chairman and managing director.

Amalgamation has long been a word that dare not speak its name in Dundee, but this might have been a good time for the two clubs to come together in some way. McLean was looking for a successor as manager and Gordon Wallace might have been the man, although Dundee FC continued their slide and were relegated at the end of season 1988–89. With a more stable business behind him, Wallace might have done better, and he did win the lower division B&Q Centenary Cup. Angus Cook was also making business improvements at Dens but it was a major, uphill task and his natural impatience meant that his business plans came to look increasingly desperate. There were rival bids for the club reported, a public flotation, changes of holding company name, an attempt to change the name of the club itself (to Dundee City) and – perhaps most audacious of all – a public £4 million bid to take over United.

Given the distribution pattern of United's shares, the bid was doomed to fail. But it was possible that Jim McLean was thinking along similar (takeover) lines, because news of another proposal involving former Dundee FC sponsor Bob Jamieson of Novaphone and the Tannadice club now surfaced, while the name of Canadian entrepeneur Ron Dixon also came out of the hat.

With boardroom matters going from bad to worse and things failing to improve on the park, Gordon Wallace took up a job as assistant manager to Jocky Scott at Dunfermline (he was replaced by Iain Munro, the former Dunfermline manager). Cook also decided to throw in his hand. His solicitor, Andrew Drummond, was reported to have taken on a 29.9 per cent share, 52.1 per cent went to two unnamed investment companies and Robert Prentice, a nephew of former manager John Prentice, became a director.

These were truly dark blue days – subsequent information via court cases and the like would reveal just how bad things were – and it is probably no exaggeration to say that the club was on the verge of extinction when Ron Dixon finally made his move in 1992. Time, of course, would reveal further chaos during his term of office, but Dixon's financial guarantees kept the banking wolves from the door and, although his jet-set, international wheeling-dealing lifestyle made for rather unorthodox football club management, a period of relative stability followed.

A business associate who had first introduced Dixon to the Dundee ice-hockey scene, Malcolm Reid, became a director at Dens and former Rangers chairman David Holmes was installed as vice-chairman. On the field, Keith Wright had moved to Hibs and Rab Shannon to Dunfermline. In had come Ian McCall, the talented ex-Ranger; and a flamboyant man of many clubs, Simon Stainrod, who soon replaced Iain Munro, first as interim player-manager and then manager when promotion was secured (1992). Dixon had made the customary noises about ground improvements – including a dog track – but Dundee FC's bite would always remain inferior to its bark if the club secured promotion and then failed to stay in the top division.

TWENTY-FIVE

All this intrigue allowed Jim McLean to get on with his own success – and succession. In 1991 he took United to another Scottish Cup final against his brother's team, Motherwell, and this time the final hurdle looked distinctly surmountable. Ex-Terror Iain Ferguson gave Motherwell the lead, but their goalkeeper Ally Maxwell suffered a rib injury which he bravely endured for the rest of the match. Bowman equalised in the second half, but Motherwell raced ahead again through O'Donnell and Angus. John O'Neil and Darren Jackson then took the tie to extra time, but a Steve Kirk winner meant the customary finale for the Arabs. United lined up: Main, Clark, Malpas, McInally, Krivokapic, Bowman, Van Der Hoorn, McKinnon (McKinlay), French, Ferguson (O'Neill), Jackson.

On the succession front, it was felt that the 'internal' candidates – Paul Sturrock (now managing St Johnstone) and Billy Kirkwood (coaching Rangers) – had yet to find the requisite managerial experience and the lucky man proved to be a Yugoslav and former captain of Red Star Belgrade, Ivan Golac. Golac had been interviewed for the Celtic job which subsequently went to Liam Brady and his appointment looked potentially a good choice for United. His affable style was in complete contrast to that of his predecessor and it was felt that an alliance of Golac's European flair on the park and McLean's hard-headedness in the boardroom might be just the ticket for the new era. The club had continued to bring through outstanding youngsters – Billy McKinlay, Duncan Ferguson and Christian Dailly – who, collectively, would add something in the region of £7 million to the Tannadice coffers. Golac negotiated at least one lucrative deal of his own – Gordan Petric, who subsequently went to Rangers for £1.5 million. Alan Main was (controversially) allowed to go to St Johnstone for £500,000 where he teamed up with Billy Dodds, signed from Dundee. Golac was also subsequently criticised by the club for ignoring its youth policy, but he will retain some kind of place in the hearts of United fans, as he achieved something which had eluded Jim McLean in six finals – the Scottish Cup. This sweet victory was achieved in 1994 against Rangers. With the Light Blues' Andy Goram missing through injury, Dailly capitalised on a mistake by Ally Maxwell to slide a shot against a post and Craig Brewster netted the rebound. United: Van de Kamp, Bowman, Malpas, Cleland, Welsh, Petric, Hannah, McInally, Brewster, McLaren, Dailly. Substitutes: Nixon and Bollan.

However, Golac's euphoria was short-lived. The very next season, his team's performance hit the skids and he was replaced by Billy Kirkwood. The ex-United player had an uphill task, though. He was unable to prevent relegation (Dundee FC also went down) and the Tannadice club – for the first time in 20 years – was entering a period of uncertainty.

Kirkwood secured promotion via the play-offs at the end of the following season, but the early-season Premier League form which followed was disappointing and he was replaced by Jim McLean's brother Tommy late in 1996. Tom had enjoyed a good career as a player with Rangers and as a manager with Motherwell and Hearts. He had actually agreed to manage Raith Rovers, but the pull of Tannadice was strong and, with a new group of Scandinavian players in place, his first season was a great success, restoring United to third in the League and thereby returning them to Europe.

Dundee FC in this period (1992–97) had also had their ups and downs. Following a welcome return to the game as a player with Partick Thistle, Jim Duffy had coached Airdrie and managed Falkirk, before rejoining the Dark Blues as a coach. He then returned to the playing staff, teaming up with some of Stainrod's excellent foreign signings such as Morten Wieghorst, Dariusz Adamczuk and Dusan Vrto as well as some young discoveries including Neil McCann, Jim Hamilton and Iain Anderson. Duffy would, in time, succeed Stainrod and lead the club to a League Cup final from the First Division, in 1995. Dundee FC: Pageaud, J. Duffy, McQueen, Manley, Wieghorst, N. Duffy, Shaw, Vrto (Farningham), Tosh (Britton), Hamilton, McCann (Anderson). Seventeen thousand Dundee fans travelled to Hampden. Aberdeen won the game 2–0, but the general signs were good and Duffy was attracting attention as a young manager. Late in 1996 he departed for Hibs (in Tom Farmer's helicopter). His successor was his assistant, John McCormack.

If the team could not capture and hold a place in the Premier League, Ron Dixon could not, realistically, be expected get the business right. The 1992 share issue was a very modest success; directors and management came and went; Andrew Drummond appeared to have his own revolving door; and police had to enter the fray at one point as Dixon and Cook swapped claim and counter claim. The Canadian regularly tried to find a buyer – at one point Malcolm Reid and Jim Duffy were said to be interested, then a Nigerian 'Prince' was in the frame – but the £2 million asking price seemed steep. At the beginning of 1997, and with a large legal settlement pending to former marketing manager Derek Souter, the club was, once again, in a fairly desperate position.

There now arrived on the Dens Park scene two brothers, local men Peter and Jimmy Marr, who had made money through pubs, retirement homes and property. They had successfully managed a local junior side, St Joseph's, with former Dundee FC player Kenny Cameron as coach. Like many before them, the businessmen were said to be interested in buying Dundee FC if the price was right, but this approach somehow seemed more professional and substantial than before. By April 1997 Dixon's 72 per cent share had changed hands for £1.35 million, with Jimmy Marr taking over as chairman, Peter Marr as vice-chair and chief executive and Derek Souter in a marketing role. Peter Marr described the time as 'the start of an important new period in the club's history'.

John McCormack was confirmed as manager and given a new contract. He failed to gain promotion in 1997, but was thought to have a promising young team. He quickly established them at the top of the First Division in the new season, winning a Bell's Manager of the Month award along the way. He would also sign a physically powerful young goalkeeper from Livingston – Rab Douglas – and a good young striker, James Grady from Clydebank. Tommy McLean was having equal success in the top flight and added Skoldmark, Andersson and Siggi Jonsson to the existing Scandinavian contingent which included Olofsson, Pedersen and Zetterlund, before taking the club to the Coca-Cola Cup final. United team was: Dykstra, Skoldmark (McSwegan 56), Malpas, Pressley, Perry, Pedersen, Olofsson, Zetterlund, Winters, Easton, Bowman.

This game was lost 3–0 to Celtic, and Trabzonspor of Turkey had eliminated the Terrors from the UEFA Cup, but

generally speaking, those in charge at Tannadice could take
some comfort from the way things were going, on and off
the park. The ground improvements were now complete,
giving Tannadice an all-seated capacity of 14,200. Such
stadium developments were now assuming greater
significance, as a new ten-team breakaway Premier League
was being discussed by the top teams. Members' grounds
would be required to have a capacity of 10,000, all-seated,
by July 1999.

This fact was obviously concentrating the mind of Peter
Marr. His team, though on top of the league at the beginning
of 1998 were beginning to show a loss of form and Marr
now proceeded to demonstrate the ruthlessness – or vision –
which would characterise his reign. With Dundee FC five
points clear of their nearest rivals, John McCormack was
sacked and replaced by Jocky Scott, who had recently taken
a coaching position with United. Even the football world –
so used to fickle boardroom behaviour – was shocked, but
the decision, said Marr, 'was made in the interest of the
club's future'. Dundee FC needed not only promotion, but a
structure which would keep them in the new Premier
League. Jocky Scott, with Jimmy Bone as assistant, duly
delivered that promotion. The boardroom pot was kept
boiling when McCormack arrested one of the club's larger
gate receipts in order to force a financial settlement, but the
Dundee FC revolution was well and truly under way. Marr
was said to be ready to spend £5 million on a new Dens
Park. He was known to prefer the idea of a completely new
stadium which might be shared with United, but feasibility
studies had revealed a financial shortfall and apparent
ambivalence from United on such a move. So Dens and
Tannadice it was. A move to the Coup was described as
'rubbish'.

Jim McLean had other things on his mind. The
shareholding of the late George Fox had become the

subject of dispute between the United chairman and his predecessor's family and, since the current directors only controlled around 50 per cent of the total, the ultimate destination of Fox's quota was important in terms of power. There was another problem. A group of United fans, unhappy with what was perceived as a slow, steady decline, called for a re-allocation of shares, the introduction of new faces to the Board and improvement in the club's public relations. United for Change (UfC), as they were known, were led by a cross section of prominent fans including Labour peer (Lord) Mike Watson and Dundee University Faculty Dean Rab Lyon, and in dialogue with a wealthy local retailer, Eddie Thompson. Jim McLean's view was that such change – including a cash injection of £1 million – would not make a significant difference to United's plight and the two sides looked set for a war of attrition.

The club avoided relegation in 1997–98 but Tommy McLean was soon under pressure again when the team went out of the Coca-Cola Cup to Ross County. Alloa had put out Dundee FC and their general start was arguably worse than United's; but perception and underlying confidence is everything in these circumstances and, as Jocky's team dug in, Tommy reached the end of the road. He was replaced by Paul Sturrock, who immediately put the finishing touches to a swap deal – Robbie Winters to Aberdeen, Billy Dodds to United – which brought not only new expectations to Tannadice, but also some cash. Sturrock's United pedigree and managerial performance at St Johnstone suggested that he was Jim McLean's natural successor. His work would be cut out, however. At the turn of 1999 the club sat ninth out of ten, with Dundee FC eighth.

Meanwhile it was not only the Dark Blues' league position which occupied the thoughts of Chairman Marr. The chief executive of the embryonic Scottish Premier League, Roger Mitchell, was beginning to fill the media space previously occupied by the legendary SFA administrator Jim Farry and, both publicly and privately, he was 'threatening' Dundee FC with exclusion from the new set-up if there were no signs of ground improvement.

Marr continued to maintain that the requisite work would begin in March, but evidence that the finance might not be in place appeared on 16 February when 'informal talks' were reported between Dundee FC and United. An *Evening Telegraph* telephone poll revealed, 58 per cent of 2,647 fans contacted favoured some kind of amalgamation. Marr said that, in spite of his investment, a £500,000 loss had been sustained in the previous financial year and only half the break-even figure of 6,000 fans were being attracted to home games. My own feeling was that the poll probably canvassed the more casual supporters. Both Norrie Price of DFC Supporters' Association and Mike Watson of UfC were sceptical of the idea, although Price thought it might be revisited further down the line and Watson thought ground-sharing a possibility.

United at least acknowledged a 'respect' between the two chairmen – an advance on previous situations – but Jim McLean was soon to pour cold water on any suggestion of a merger. There was no way it would take shape at that time, he said: ground-sharing was not a legal option as things stood; although he believed there should only be one team in the city, United had spent £7 million on ground improvements and had a healthy balance sheet, so the clubs were not equal on that basis; and, all things considered, United would only consider a takeover (of DFC, by DUFC).

Such candour was welcome, but it left Dundee FC needing £1.2 million of a total cost of £2.93 million. A further share issue was launched, seeking £400,000. A 'brick sale' was suggested which might raise another £100,000. And Dundee fans were asked to turn up in

numbers for the next game, against St Johnstone. Seven
thousand responded. The team lost 1–0.

All this suddenly paled into insignificance the following
week, however, when it was announced that the club had
been sold to an Anglo-Italian businessman, Giovanni Di
Stefano, who reportedly had links to Serbian genocide
squads. The Marrs denied it, but admitted that they had been
contacted by the man – his son, a Gordonstoun pupil, had
apparently read of Dundee's plight – who had offered £1
million. It got worse. Not only did Di Stefano acknowledge
business links with the notorious Arkan, a warlord cited by
the US State Department for Serbian crimes during the
Bosnian conflict, he cheerfully admitted to having met
Saddam Hussein and to admiring Mussolini (and, curiously,
Alex Salmond). He had also been jailed briefly in the UK
for fraud before being released on appeal.

The Marrs were clearly stuck between a rock and the
Powrie Brae. An SPL spokesman was poetically reported to
be 'seriously pissed off and not inclined to do Dundee any
favours'; the club was being tipped for relegation, thereby
making other potential investors wary; and vice-chairman
Derek Souter was said to be implacably opposed to any
involvement with Di Stefano.

Miraculously, not only did everyone see sense and ditch
Di Stefano, the Marrs managed to find the balance (£1.34
million) from more legitimate sources and work began
during March while United agreed to temporary ground-
sharing. This led to another round of amalgamation
speculation – the name Sporting Club of Dundee briefly
surfaced – and another round of pontification from the
pundits: 'There is no such thing as merger,' said journalist
Glenn Gibbons, 'only takeover.' Bob Crampsey opined that
it was impossible in Dundee in any case, because sport was
based upon sentiment.

As it happens, I don't agree with either of these

viewpoints, although I don't underestimate the Dundee problem. The Inverness case disproves the first point and the fact that sentiment is not genetically transmitted suggests that a new (successful) club would do well, with some fans initially and with more as time went on. Footballing success is the key.

However, Peter Marr was now said to have disposed of some other assets and to be living in Majorca as a tax exile. Whether this provided the money or guarantees for Dundee FC, I am not certain, but things remained tense in the boardroom and led to Derek Souter's resignation. There was also a local rumour to the effect that United had potential investors who would only commit if there was one team in the city. On the park, meanwhile, it was United who faced the greater threat of relegation having won only two league games at home in the entire season. Jocky Scott's side won five out of its last seven games to finish fifth and Alan Pattullo of *The Scotsman* declared him to be Manager of the Season in the light of the off-field difficulties he had had to face. Dundee FC finished above United for the first time since 1974–75, when Jocky was a Dundee player.

At Tannadice, where the Terrors were now six years without a trophy, UfC offered £750,000 for Jim McLean's shareholding, stating that their sole aim was to oust the chairman. McLean, dismissing 'Eddie Thompson and his wee committee,' vowed to stay.

CONCLUSION 2000

And so the new millennium dawned. The 1990s had actually been a fairly cataclysmic final decade with the fall of Communism, murderous wars in the Gulf, the Balkans and innumerable other places; the death of Princess Diana; a Labour landslide; and a Scottish Parliament.

In football the Bosman ruling, whereby players could leave at the end of their contracts without transfer fees, had radically altered clubs' relationships with players. It had led to an influx of foreign players, some of whom graced the game but often to the exclusion of young Scots, and the complete abandonment of transfer fees was possibly now on the horizon. Rangers had won nine championships in a row before Walter Smith had handed the managerial reins over to Dutchman Dick Advocaat and the very existence of Celtic had been threatened before Fergus McCann put the club on its feet again with a new stadium and a Premier League championship under Wim Janssen. Both teams now depended heavily on quality foreign players and this trend also accelerated at other Scottish clubs.

Billy Dodds left United for Rangers and Dundee FC signed a good Italian, Patrizio Billio who, as a young man, had made the bench of AC Milan when players such as Van Basten, Gullit, Rikaard, Baresi and Paolo Maldini were on the park. Both Dundee FC and United continued to struggle, although Jocky was again in the ascendancy and, with a 'basketball back three' of Tweed, Wilkie and Ireland he managed to give Rangers their only home defeat of the season. (The club also lost thirteen goals in consecutive Old Firm matches, but we won't mention that.) The *Sporting Post* went the way of all newspapers – to the great chip shop in the sky – and, on a more serious note, the former Dundee chairman, Ian Gellatly, whose family had given long and often distinguished service to the club, died at the age of 61. Ron Dixon was also to die in a car crash in Mexico, later in the year.

The main thing from the Dundee FC fans' point of view was that Jocky was keeping them up, but the game suddenly took a change of direction when it was revealed that, first, some Spanish players (including Luna and Artero) and then some English, Scottish and Australian ones would be arriving at Dens. The ghostly figure of Steve Archibald was said to be involved, as was Peter Marr. The point, of course, being that Jocky was not. His contract was known to be up in the summer but, notwithstanding what had happened to John McCormack, it was surely inconceivable that the manager would be asked to leave, given his record.

On 6 May 2000, when Dundee beat United 3–0 at Dens, it was their biggest derby win in 27 years, their first Dens derby win since 1989, and a result which would contribute to Dundee FC finishing above United in the Premier League again. In normal footballing circles, this would have been a time of crisis for the losing team. Two days later it was announced that Jocky Scott and Jimmy Bone were not to have their contracts renewed. The fans were stunned (although generally supportive of the Marrs' record), the press apoplectic. Alan Pattullo of *The Scotsman* – a most perceptive scribe where footballing matters Dundonian are involved – said that Dens, 'once perceived [during the Gellatly family era] as a port of decency', was now 'simply a home to grog house politics'. For Scott, it was 'the worst few days of my career'.

The Marrs, however, like anyone steeled in business, had made their decision and would stand by it. Scott's successors would be two Italian brothers, Ivano and Dario Bonetti, largely unknown in this country (although Ivano had played for both Tranmere and Grimsby) but with outstanding Italian footballing pedigrees. Ivano (35) had been a first-team player for Juventus, Sampdoria, Roma – he was on the books when they played United in the European Cup – and Torino and he would act as player-manager at Dens with his brother as coach. They had recently been in charge of a fifth division Italian side, Sestrese. The directors hoped the brothers would initiate a brand of football which would bring the lapsed supporters back to Dens. A bigger budget would be available to them and the plan was to get Dundee into Scotland's top three in three years. The fitness coach would be Enzo Romano and the club co-ordinator Dario Magri, who had performed a similar role under Attilio Lombardi at Crystal Palace.

In many ways, the fans did not know what to make of things at this stage, but United were certainly knocked off the sports pages over the next few months as Dundee FC signed Georgi Nemzadse, the Georgian captain; Marco di Marchi from Juve via Vitesse in Holland; Argentinian strikers Fabian Caballero and Juan Sara; and an Italian left back, Marcello Marrocco. The footballing philosophy would be a mixture of Italian and Scots, in other words intelligent, positional defence with aggressive attack; the Forthill Sports club would be the new training ground; sponsorship would come from an Italian coffee company; and pre-season training would take place in the Italian Alps. In one revealing interview, Caballero said that the English, Italian and Spanish Leagues were the best in the world and it was exciting to be close to them. One thing the Bonettis could not be faulted for was style, and 4,000 season tickets were sold for Dens – although it was a measure of United's consolidation over the years that they *still* sold *more*.

Both Ivano and Paul Sturrock were said to be approaching the new season with confidence and, on 29 July 2000, all began to be revealed. On Dundee's part, there was great promise with a stylish 2–0 win at Motherwell including an Artero wonder goal (although Bonetti went off with two yellow cards). United lost 2–1 at home to Celtic.

In game two, Dundee beat Dunfermline 3–0 at Dens, while United lost by the same score to Hibs. In fact, Hibs were a good side, but Sturrock had had enough and sensationally resigned after the match, citing ill-health. His replacement was Alex Smith, who would work with John Blackley and Maurice Malpas.

Dundee FC now topped the league and, although Ivano was not getting carried away, the fans were beginning to. Another large contingent travelled to Easter Road and, in 12 minutes, saw Dundee take a spectacular lead through Caballero. Two outstanding goals from Agathe put them behind, but the Dark Blues were still in the game when, just before half-time, Matthias Jack put in a brutal tackle against Caballero to send him flying. The Argentinian appeared to punch the German on the way down and was sent off. The game was killed and when Billio was also red-carded, Dundee went down 5–1.

These incidents were to throw the club off course. Scottish players and managers had been casting aspersions upon Latin temperament and honesty and Dundee (legitimately) complained about racial stereotyping. A plan was put in place to discuss discipline and other matters with referees and the SPL; but more controversy was to follow in games with Hearts, and St Mirren, with more sendings off. Things came to a head in the local derby, when Caballero was badly injured in a three-way clash with United's Jason de Vos and Kevin Mc Donald, but Dundee FC won the game 3–0. This maintained their top-six place as United languished at the bottom.

In early October Dundee FC announced the signing of two Argentinian internationals, Beto Carranza and – sensationally – Claudio Caniggia who, in 1990 and 1994 had formed national striking partnerships with Gabriel Batistuta and Diego Maradonna. Caniggia made his début on 14 October, at Aberdeen and scored a delightful goal in Dundee's 2–0 victory.

That day, however, would be remembered in the City of Dundee for something even more dramatic. United, lying bottom of the Premier League, lost 4–0 at home to Hearts. In a post-match interview, chairman Jim McLean once again lost control of himself and assaulted a BBC reporter. He immediately took the decision to resign as chairman and managing director and thus ended an important chapter in the history of professional football in the city. It was a desperately sad conclusion to a career which had brought great honour and no little excitement to the 'City of Discovery'.

BIBLIOGRAPHY

H.B. Boyne, *Dark Blue Down the Years*. Simmath Press.
——————— *Dundee United FC Through the Years*. Simmath Press.

R. Brasch, *How Did Sports Begin?* Longman.

John Cottrell, *A Century of Great Soccer Drama*.

Jimmy Guthrie, *Soccer Rebel*.

John Hutchison, *The Football Industry*. Richard Drew.

J.M. Jackson (ed.), *The City of Dundee*. The Third Statistical Account of Scotland, 1977.

S.J. Jones (ed.), *Dundee & District*. British Association.

B. Lenman and K. Donaldson, 'Partners, Incomes, Investments and Diversification in the Scottish Linen Area'. *Business History* XIII, No. 1 (18), 1971.

William McGonagall, *More Poetic Gems*. Duckworth.

Tony Mason, *Association Football and English Society 1863–1915*. Stanley Paul.

James Michener, *On Sport*. Secker & Warburg.

D. Phillips, *Jimmy Shand: A Biography*. Winter.

John Prebble, *The High Girders*. Secker & Warburg.

Norrie Price, *Up Wi' the Bonnets*. Self-published.

John Rafferty, *One Hundred Years of Scottish Football*. Pan Books.

John Ramsden, *The Age of Balfour and Baldwin*, Vol. 3 in *The History of the Conservative Party*. Longman.

D.S. Riddell, *Leisure (1961)*. The Third Statistical Account of Scotland, 1977.

Forrest Robertson (ed.), *Mackinlay's A–Z of Scottish Football*. MacDonald Publishers.

Scottish Football Association, 1878–79, *The Scottish Football Annual of the Scottish Football Association*.

William M. Walker, *Juteopolis: Dundee and its Textile Workers 1885–1923*. Scottish Academic Press.

Mike Watson, *Rags to Riches*. Winter.

The following periodicals have proved invaluable sources for the research of this book:

NEWSPAPERS

The Advertiser
The Courier
The Courier and Advertiser
Daily Record
Dundee Evening Telegraph and Post
Glasgow Herald
The Glasgow Observer
The Guardian
The People's Journal
The Scotsman
Scottish Referee
Scottish Sport
Scottish Umpire
Sport Illustrated
The Sporting Post
Sunday Mail
Sunday Post
The Sunday Standard
The Sunday Times

OTHERS

Dundee and Round About
The Dundee Directory
The Dundee FC Programme
The Dundee United FC Programme
The Dundee United Handbook
Who's Who of Scottish Internationalists